MIKE LEIGH

INTERVIEWS

CONVERSATIONS WITH FILMMAKERS SERIES
PETER BRUNETTE, GENERAL EDITOR

Photofest

MIKE
LEIGH

INTERVIEWS

EDITED BY HOWIE MOVSHOVITZ

UNIVERSITY PRESS OF MISSISSIPPI / JACKSON

www.upress.state.ms.us

08 07 06 05 04 03 02 01 00   4 3 2 1

∞

Library of Congress Cataloging-in-Publication Data
Leigh, Mike, 1943-
    Mike Leigh: interviews / edited by Howie Movshovitz.
        p. cm.—(Conversations with filmmakers series)
    Filmography: p.
    Includes index.
    ISBN 1-57806-067-2 (cloth : alk. paper).—ISBN 1-57806-068-0
    (paper : alk. paper)
    1. Leigh, Mike, 1943–   . 2. Motion picture producers and directors—
Great Britain Interviews.   I. Movshovitz, Howie.
II. Title. III. Series.
IN PROCESS
791.43'0233'092—dc21   99-44200
    [B]   CIP

British Library Cataloging-in-Publication data available

CONTENTS

INTRODUCTION

DURING THE RUN OF his play, *A Rancid Pong,* in August, 1971, Mike Leigh was contacted by London's *Evening News* for a brief item about the filming of Leigh's earlier play, *Bleak Moments*. This would be Leigh's first film. He was then known—at least to the *Evening News*—as *Michael* Leigh, but two things stand out in that early notice: Leigh was already known as an improviser, and he had a sharp tongue. Describing an early play at a Catholic teacher training school, Leigh said, "It was a women's college. We did a play about a priest cracking up. There was quite an outcry over that."

Interviewers have been asking Leigh about how he puts films together ever since, as if he will always be suspected of somehow undermining the good order of the cinema by unleashing the forces of chaos. In 1977, he tells Sheridan Morley of *The Times* of London, "I believe in improvisation within a structured surrounding; this is not some kind of all-in anarchic democracy." While one might hear a touch of defensiveness in that answer, over the course of these interviews the issue seems to be more that Leigh is an extremely ordered man. His discussion of his work is always as careful and precise as the work itself. Leigh tells Peter Brunette in 1991 that it took three months of rehearsal and another nine weeks of shooting to produce *Life Is Sweet*. "I write a structure that is very brief," Leigh says, "like three pages . . . And each scene is built and rehearsed on location and built up through lots of rehearsal until it's ready and then it gets shot."

The question of what caused Leigh to develop his unique approach to filmmaking also gets different—yet complementary—answers. Leigh tells

Judy Block that his experiences with a Zionist youth group—and their camping trips—made him aware of the value of cooperative endeavors. When speaking with Mirra Bank, Leigh talks about the influence of John Cassavetes's improvised 1959 *Shadows,* and also his reaction against his time at RADA (The Royal Aacdemy of Dramatic Art), where he "trained as an actor in the most sterile atmosphere." Bank's interview is particularly interesting because she has known Mike Leigh for many years and is able to bring his attention to a number of formative experiences—his love for BBC Radio's *Goon Show,* his interest in writer Flann O'Brien, and his comment that even while he worked exclusively in the theater in the 1960s, it was *"always* with a view to making films."

These interviews reveal that it was also always with a view to getting as close to actuality as is possible by means of dramatic film. Leigh admits several times that his films are partly caricatures, but the goal is nevertheless reality. "My films," Leigh tells Kenneth Turan, "aspire to the condition of documentary."

Filmmakers don't do interviews because they love to talk about their work with strangers. They do interviews because they want to promote their films. For the most part, when filmmakers are writing or directing, or even just hoping to develop a project, they don't want to be bothered, and it's rare to be able to speak with a filmmaker during those times. The reader may notice that the interviews in this book, reprinted as originally published, tend to cluster around the releases of Mike Leigh's films. And the American interviews, at least, also mark the times when Leigh chose to be available. He spoke to critics from around the world about *Naked* at the International Film Festival at Cannes in 1994, and he came to the United States in 1996 to do interviews for the release of *Secrets & Lies.* Leigh didn't come to the U.S. for many of his earlier films nor to promote *Career Girls* in 1997, and so the American interview record is spare on those projects.

The way interviews are done gives them a particular character. The good ones have the intensity of what should be a lengthy conversation squeezed into—at best—an hour, often in a hotel room or another spot grabbed on the run. And interviews often cover the same ground because in the world of daily journalism, the "issue" of a film is often defined quickly and in advance (by the film itself, the publicists, editors, or whatever mysterious force identifies such things), and the rush of events makes it difficult for interviews to take any other course. The first time I met Leigh we spoke in the back of a hotel restaurant on the beach at Cannes where the staff were gearing up for lunch. Dishes and trays clattered, while waiters rushed by and called to one another (the tape was useless for radio). The next time, we sat at a pair of children's desks in the quiet but echo-y basement of an elementary school in Telluride, Colorado, between film screenings at the Telluride Film Festival. That tape was useless also. Of all the interviews in this book, only the longer pieces by Kenneth Turan of the *Los Angeles Times,* Richard Porton and Lee Ellickson of the film magazine *Cineaste,* Judy Bloch for the Pacific Film Archive, and Mirra Bank for *Films in Review* were done with any sense of leisure and comfort.

But the hurried moments can yield comments and information every bit as revealing and useful to the understanding of this remarkable film-maker as the calmer discussions captured in the longer articles. During those brief interviews, filmmakers are usually "on" with a unique level of energy. Leigh will answer the same questions with different sets of words and shifts of nuance, or with different examples. And the result may clarify a difficult point, add information to something which was incomplete, or show that Leigh's ideas are fluid rather than rigid. The more Leigh talks about the unconventional way he grows his films through lengthy improvisations and rehearsals with his actors, the more it becomes clear that Leigh has obviously refined his approach, and that with each film the process works somewhat differently from the others.

Leigh began his career as a maker of plays—the word *playwright* doesn't quite fit an artist who does so much in collaboration with his actors—and he entered filmmaking with perhaps more practical experience with stage-craft than with cinema. But that began to change, and as Leigh says to Judy Bloch in 1991, "To be honest, I found long rehearsals, investigating the relationships, the research, endlessly fascinating, and in some respects I find it something of a chore now. Having said that, what I find ever increasingly delightful and pleasurable is the process of actual filming." A bit later, it's particularly refreshing when Ray Pride reports that Leigh, perhaps annoyed, once told an audience in an after-the-play discussion that he really doesn't care about the "process"—it's the result that matters.

In Donn Pennebaker's documentary *Don't Look Back,* singer Bob Dylan is asked what his songs are about, to which Dylan responds with something like, "Some are about five or six minutes and some are about eight or nine minutes." Alfred Hitchcock, we're often told, simply lied to interviewers. It's always good to keep in mind that when artists talk about their own work, there's usually the sense behind their comments that their films (or songs) are—or should be—self-explanatory.

I don't believe that Mike Leigh hides himself the way Hitchcock and Dylan do, but if one reads the interviews carefully, one sees that Leigh's comments and explanations shift not only with time, but also with the circumstances. With most of the interviews in this book, we don't know where the conversation took place, what the weather was, whether the coffee was any good, or what things were said that aren't included in the written work. Most of the time, we also don't know what questions were asked. The published interviews are shaped by the individual writers, who have their own ideas about what Mike Leigh is doing in his films and what kind of person he is. But it's also obvious that Leigh responds differently to different interviewers. In some interviews he's warmer, more forthcoming, more expansive. For whatever reasons, from one interview to the next, Leigh has greater—or lesser—trust in the interviewer's knowledge, under- standing, and intentions. But, again, these differences make for equally interesting reading by giving us multiple perspectives on particular ideas and films.

Perhaps the most common phrase used by those who have interviewed Mike Leigh is that "he doesn't suffer fools gladly." In addition to a number of interviewers, the actress Alison Steadman, Leigh's former wife, uses that very phrase when explaining to Kenneth Turan how Leigh behaves in inter- views. Another interviewer, who did not want his piece reprinted, said that he and Leigh got into a spat and the interview didn't go anywhere. But while you hear—and read—that Leigh is a bear to interview, that reputa- tion doesn't pan out in what he says in these pages, or in the comments of many of the writers in this book. Turan, a great champion of Mike Leigh's films, loved talking to Leigh, as did Peter Brunette, David Sterritt, and oth- ers with whom I've spoken personally about their experience. I've found Leigh comfortable and open in conversation, and expansive.

Leigh's comments are often spicy and sharp-edged, which may frighten or alarm some interviewers (and readers), and he seems always to assume and demand, that an interviewer be prepared and show some genuine frame of reference and knowledge of film—and of the world in general. He expects interviewers to be thoughtful and ready to think. While he knows that certain questions are inevitable, he'll reject or give short shrift to a question carelessly put, and in my experience he seems to demand that an interviewer stay with the train of thought, wherever it leads.

In his good and useful biography of Mike Leigh, *The World According to Mike Leigh* (HarperCollins, London, 1996), Michael Coveney quotes Leigh's response to a questionnaire from the London magazine *City Limits*:

> *His perfect night out? Food, film, fuck.*
> *The one film he would choose to see again: (Truffaut's)* Les Quatre Cents Coups
> *If he was a pigeon, who would he crap on? Whoever wrote this question-naire.*
> *Epitaph? "Mike Leigh. Warmed up 1943. Came out of character (sometime in the next century)."*

In the British/American comedy *Notting Hill*, there's a terrific parody of press junkets for movies, with Hugh Grant suddenly finding himself in the middle of one of those hotel interview fiascoes as the writer from *Horse and Hound* magazine. He winds up doing a series of hasty interviews with the cast of a new film, and he figures things out quickly—he asks all the formulaic (and finally disinterested) press junket questions about actors identifying with characters and preparing for roles.

You wouldn't want to ask those questions of Mike Leigh, who would surely turn them right back on the questioner. But with sensible, intelligent, and interested questions, Leigh is exceptionally good to engage in conversation.

I find it fascinating that the now-standard question for Mike Leigh about his "process," leads to many other questions and ideas. It connects to conversations about wealth and social class, or the British film industry, the financing of films, and sometimes personal matters of family and religion, and these too change over time. To Judy Stone, Leigh talks about Jewish issues in terms of Zionist activities, but six years later, to Kenneth Turan, Leigh describes the deeper manifestation of his religious and cultural background: "The tragicomic view of life, if you know what you're talking about, there's a Jewish flavor to it, a Jewishness in the spirit of it."

As of this writing, Mike Leigh is at the height of his career. He's respected around the world, although still more in the United States and France than in his own country, and while *Career Girls* was received less well than earlier films, there's been steady progression in appreciation and attention from *High Hopes,* to *Life Is Sweet, Naked,* and *Secrets & Lies.*

Equally important, Leigh has become an important talker about film. Plenty of filmmakers, whose work is respected, have little to say that adds to our understanding of the nature and possibilities of cinema. Mike Leigh has a great deal to say about those things. He's brought to the cinema an unusual way of creating films, which expands the medium and makes everyone who sees his films question their own assumptions—about Leigh's films, their own work, and the cinema itself. Best of all, for a book based on talk, Mike Leigh is a great talker.

CHRONOLOGY

1902   Leigh's grandfather, Mayer Liebermann, emigrates from Russia to England.

1943   Born in Salford, England, a Manchester suburb, on February 20.

1960   Wins scholarship to RADA (Royal Academy of Dramatic Art).

1963   Studies painting and drawing at Camberwell School of Art in London.

1964   Enrolls in night class at London School of Film Technique.

1965   Production of *The Box Play,* his first.

1970   Stage production of *Bleak Moments,* March 16 at Open Space Theatre, London.

1971   Production of the film *Bleak Moments,* his first feature.

1973   Marries Alison Steadman.

1977   First stage production of *Abigail's Party,* April 11 at Hampstead Theatre, London.

1980   *Grown-Ups* becomes the first made-for-television movie admitted to the London Film Festival.

1988   *High Hopes,* Leigh's second theatrical feature film, screens at the New York Film Festival.

1989   Leigh and Simon Channing-Williams form Thin Man Films.

1993   Named "best director" at Cannes for *Naked.* David Thewlis is named "best actor."

1996   *Secrets & Lies* wins Palme d'Or at Cannes.

1997   Nominated for an Academy Award (U.S.) as best director for *Secrets & Lies.*

FILMOGRAPHY*

1971
BLEAK MOMENTS
Autumn Productions/Memorial Enterprises/BFI Production Board
Producer/editor: Les Blair
Cinematographer: Bahram Manoochehri
Production designer: Richard Rambaut
Sound: Bob Withey
Cast: Anne Raitt (Sylvia), Sarah Stephenson (Hilda), Eric Allan (Peter), Joolia Cappleman (Pat), Mike Bradwell (Norman)
III minutes

1973
HARD LABOUR
BBC TV
Producer: Tony Garnett
Cinematographer: Tony Pierce-Roberts
Editor: Christopher Rowlands
Sound: Dick Manton
Production designer: Paul Munting
Costumes: Sally Nieper
Cast: Liz Smith (Mrs. Thornley), Clifford Kershaw (Mr. Thornley), Polly Hemingway (Ann), Bernard Hill (Edward), Alison Steadman (Veronica),

*Unless noted, all films are written and directed by Mike Leigh.

Vanessa Harris (Mrs. Stone), Cyril Varley (Mr. Stone), Linda Beckett (Julie), Ben Kingsley (Naseem)
75 minutes

1975
THE FIVE MINUTE FILMS
BBC TV (broadcast 1982)
Producer: Tony Garnett
Cinematographer: Brian Tufano
Editor: Chris Lovett
Sound: Andrew Boulton

Casts:

The Birth of the 2001 F.A. Cup Final Goalie
Richard Ireson (Father), Celia Quicke (Mother)

Old Chums
Tim Sterne (Brian), Robert Putt (Terry)

Probation
Herbert Norville (Arbley), Billy Colvill (Sid), Anthony Carrick (Mr. Davies), Theresa Watson (Secretary), Lally Percy (Victoria)

A Light Snack
Margaret Heery (Mrs. White), Richard Griffiths (window-cleaner), Alan Gaunt (talker), David Casey (listener)

Afternoon
Rachel Davies (hostess), Pauline Moran (teacher), Julie North (newly-wed)

25 minutes

1976
NUTS IN MAY
BBC TV
Producer: David Rose
Cinematographer: Michael Williams
Editor: Oliver White
Sound: John Gilbert
Production designer: David Crozier

Costumes: Gini Hardy
Cast: Roger Sloman (Keith), Alison Steadman (Candice-Marie), Anthony
O'Donnell (Ray), Sheila Kelley (Honky), Stephen Bill (Finger), Richenda
Carey (Miss Beale), Eric Allan (quarryman), Matthew Guinness (farmer),
Sally Watts (farm girl), Richard Ireson (policeman)
80 minutes

1977
THE KISS OF DEATH
BBC TV
Producer: David Rose
Cinematographers: Michael Williams and John Kenway
Editor: Oliver White
Production designer: David Crozier
Sound: John Gilbert
Music: Al Barnett
Costumes: Al Barnett
Cast: David Threlfall (Trevor), Clifford Kershaw (Mr. Garside), John
Wheatley (Ronnie), Pamela Austin (Trevor's mother), Angela Curran
(Sandra), Phillip Ryland (Froggy), Kay Adshead (Linda)
80 minutes

1979
WHO'S WHO
BBC TV
Producer: Margaret Matheson
Cinematographer: John Else
Editor: Chris Lovett
Production designer: Austen Spriggs
Costumes: Robin Stubbs
Sound: John Pritchard
Cast: Simon Chandler (Nigel), Adam Norton (Giles), Richard Kane (Alan),
Jeffrey Wiclham (Francis), Souad Faress (Samya), Philip Davis (Kevin),
Graham Seed (Anthony), Joolia Cappleman (April), Lavinia Bertram
(Nancy), Francesca Martin (Selina), David Neville (Lord Crouchhurst),
Richenda Carey (Lady Crouchhurst)
80 minutes

1980
GROWN-UPS
BBC TV
Producer: Louis Marks
Cinematographer: Remi Adefarasin
Editor: Robin Sales
Production designer: Bryan Ellis
Costumes: Christian Dyall
Sound: John Pritchard
Cast: Philip Davis (Dick), Lesley Manville (Mandy), Brenda Blethyn
(Gloria), Janine Duvitski (Sharon), Lindsay Duncan (Christine), Sam Kelley
(Ralph)
90 minutes

1982
HOME SWEET HOME
BBC TV
Producer: Louis Marks
Cinematographer: Remi Adefarasin
Editor: Robin Sales
Production designer: Bryan Ellis
Costumes: Michael Burdle
Sound: John Pritchard
Music: Carl Davis
Cast: Timothy Spall (Gordon), Eric Richard (Stan), Tim Barker (Harold),
Kay Stonham (Hazel), Su Elliott (June), Frances Barber (Melody), Sheila
Kelley (Janice), Lorraine Brunning (Tina), Heidi Laratta (Kelly)
90 minutes

1983
MEANTIME
Central Television/Mostpoint Ltd. for Channel 4
Producer: Graham Benson
Cinematographer: Roger Pratt
Editor: Lesley Walker
Production designer: Diana Charnley
Costumes: Lindy Hemming

Sound: Malcolm Hirst
Music: Andrew Dickson
Cast: Marion Bailey (Barbara), Phil Daniels (Mark), Tim Roth (Colin), Pam
Ferris (Mavis), Jeff Robert (Frank), Alfred Molina (John), Gary Oldman
(Coxy), Tilly Vosburgh (Hayley), Paul Daly (Rusty), Leila Bertrand (Hayley's
friend), Hepburn Graham (boyfriend)
90 minutes

1985
FOUR DAYS IN JULY
BBC TV
Producer: Kenith Trodd
Cinematographer: Remi Adefarasin
Editor: Robin Sales
Production designer: Jim Clay
Costumes: Maggie Donnelly
Sound: John Pritchard
Music: Rachel Portman
Cast: Brid Brennan (Collette), Des McAleer (Eugene), Paula Hamilton
(Lorraine), Charles Lawson (Billy), Brian Hogg (Big Billy), Adrian Gordon
(Little Billy), Shane Connaughton (Brendan), Eileen Pollock (Carmel),
Stephen Rea (Dixie)
96 minutes

1987
THE SHORT AND CURLIES
Film Four/Portman
Producers: Victor Glynn and Simon Channing-Williams
Cinematographer: Roger Pratt
Editor: Jon Gregory
Production designer: Diana Charnley
Costumes: Lindy Hemming
Sound: Malcolm Hirst
Music: Rachel Portman
Cast: David Thewlis (Clive), Alison Steadman (Betty), Sylvestra Le Touzel
(Joy), Wendy Nottingham (Charlene)
18 minutes

1988
HIGH HOPES
Film Four International/British Screen/Portman
Producers: Simon Channing-Williams and Victor Glynn
Cinematographer: Roger Pratt
Editor: John Gregory
Production designer: Diana Charnley
Costumes: Lindy Hemming
Sound: Billy McCarthy
Music: Andrew Dickson
Cast: Philip Davis (Cyril), Ruth Sheen (Shirley), Edna Doré (Mrs. Bender),
Heather Tobias (Valerie), Philip Jackson (Martin), Lesley Manville
(Laetitia), David Bamber (Rupert), Jason Watkins (Wayne), Judith Scott
(Suzi)
110 minutes

1990
LIFE IS SWEET
Thin Man/Film Four International/British Screen
Producer: Simon Channing-Williams
Cinematographer: Dick Pope
Editor: Jon Gregory
Production designer: Alison Chitty
Costumes: Lindy Hemming
Sound: Malcolm Hirst
Music: Rachel Portman
Cast: Alison Steadman (Wendy), Jim Broadbent (Andy), Claire Skinner
(Natalie), Jane Horrocks (Nicola), Timothy Spall (Aubrey), Stephen Rea
(Patsy), David Thewlis (Nicola's lover), Moya Brady (Paula), David Neilson
(Steve), Harriet Thorpe (customer), Paul Trussell (chef)
102 minutes

1992
A SENSE OF HISTORY
Thin Man/Film Four International
Producer: Simon Channing-Williams
Screenwriter: Jim Broadbent

Cinematographer: Dick Pope
Production designer: Alison Chitty
Sound: Tim Fraser
Music: Carl David
Cast: Jim Broadbent (23rd Earl of Leete), Stephen Bill (Giddy)
28 minutes

1993
NAKED
Thin Man/Film Four International/British Screen
Producer: Simon Channing-Williams
Cinematographer: Dick Pope
Editor: Jon Gregory
Production designer: Alison Chitty
Costumes: Lindy Hemming
Sound: Ken Weston
Music: Andrew Dickson
Cast: David Thewlis (Johnny), Lesley Sharp (Louise), Katrin Cartledge
(Sophie), Greg Cruttwell (Jeremy), Claire Skinner (Sandra), Peter Wight
(Brian), Ewen Bremner (Archie), Susan Vidler (Maggie)
126 minutes

1996
SECRETS AND LIES
Channel Four Films/CiBy 2000/Thin Man Productions
Producer: Simon Channing-Williams
Music: Andrew Dickson
Cinematographer: Dick Pope
Editor: Jon Gregory
Production designer: Alison Chitty
Costumes: Maria Price
Cast: Timothy Spall (Maurice), Phyllis Logan (Monica), Brenda Blethyn
(Cynthia), Claire Rushbrook (Roxanne), Marianne Jean-Baptiste
(Hortense), Elizabeth Berrington (Jane), Michele Austin (Dionne), Lee Ross
(Paul), Lesley Manville (social worker), Ron Cook (Stuart), Emma Amos
(girl with scar)
136 minutes

1997
CAREER GIRLS
Matrix Film and Television Partnership/Channel Four Films and Thin Man
Productions
Producer: Simon Channing-Williams
Cinematographer: Dick Pope
Editor: Robin Sales
Sound: George Richards
Music: Marianne Jean-Baptiste and Tony Remy
Production design and costumes: Eve Stewart
Cast: Katrin Cartlidge (Hannah), Lynda Steadman (Annie), Kate Byers
(Claire), Mark Benton (Ricky), Andy Serkis (Mr. Evans), Joe Tucker (Adrian),
Margo Stanley (Ricky's Nan), Michael Healy (Lecturer)
87 minutes

MIKE LEIGH

INTERVIEWS

Mike Leigh: Anything But Anarchy

SHERIDAN MORLEY/1977

ABIGAIL'S PARTY (WHICH REOPENS at the Hampstead Theatre on Monday after an initial and critically-acclaimed run there earlier in the year) is by general reckoning the nearest the English theatre has lately come to the intense hosts-versus-guests...despair...of Albee's *Virginia Woolf*. It has also been the most remarkable recent success of a theatre currently enjoying a winning streak. But what separates *Abigail's Party* from the general round is that it appears not to have been written at all: instead, it has been "devised" by the 34-year-old stage and film director Mike Leigh.

Apart from his film and television work, Leigh has been responsible for more than thirty plays in the last 10 years, many devised and put together in circumstances resembling those at Hampstead. "I believe in improvisation within a structured surrounding: this is not some kind of all-in anarchic democracy. At Hampstead I had the promise of a specified number of actors and nine rehearsal weeks: I also knew roughly the dimensions of the Hampstead stage and the likely sort of audience you find there, but that, up to the first day of rehearsal, was all I had to work with."

On the first day of rehearsal, it is Leigh's custom to approach each actor (many of whom he will have worked with before) and ask them to find a character.

"Generally they come up with a list of five or six friends, people they would like to be, and during the first week or two of rehearsal I then work

---

From *The Times* (London), 15 July 1977. © Sheridan Morley/Times Newspapers Limited, 1977. Reprinted by permission.

independently with each of the actors until he or she has selected one: these are not acting exercises in which people are supposed to be funny or inventive or amusing—they're a genuine search for characters who are then researched and built into a final script. Characters develop, then relationships, and these I monitor and follow and push towards a dramatic conflict of some kind, so that you get a microcosm of society through improvisation. At one point in the *Abigail's Party* rehearsals we had three quite separate themes going, and the occasion of the play was the interrelation of those themes. On paper the quality of the piece isn't great: what makes it work is I think the unstated tensions and implications which have grown up during a long rehearsal period. The final draft of the play wasn't complete and didn't really exist until the first night, though now the alterations from night to night are very few.

"But as soon as you start talking about improvisation people expect anarchy: in fact our objectives in *Abigail's Party,* the things we wanted to say about these people and their social habits and surroundings, remained rock solid from the very first: only the surface text is flexible.

"A great many actors find it impossible to work like this: the ability to improvise intelligently is not the same as the old Rep actors' ability to ad lib in a crisis. The actor here has to think only of his own character: once he starts worrying about the overall framework of the play or if it'll work, then he's lost: it's only really good for actors who want to play real people instead of stage characters. Improvising has nothing to do with writhing and twitching or exploring an arty process for its own sake: what we're trying here is a form of social documentary."

After RADA (where he was in the generation of David Halliwell, Ian McShane, David Warner and Sarah Miles) Leigh went to be an assistant stage manager in Rep at Leatherhead until he got a plug thrust in his eye and was taken to hospital. From there he went into films, in the days when there were still such things as B pictures:

"Everyone wore 10 feet of make-up and they used to construct entire transport cafés on the set because nobody had apparently yet thought of filming in a real one: I got a few bit parts and a good job as a deaf mute in a *Maigret* episode but then I jacked it in and went to the Camberwell school of art because I was interested in design. There, in a life drawing class, I suddenly realized what it was I'd always hated about RADA: we never made an organic or truthful statement about what we were experiencing—everything was secondhand or borrowed or learnt. Nobody ever confronted themselves with in-the-street experience, or tried to distil or express it. Now you will find the importance of all that in Stanislavsky, but to me it was a revelation: suddenly you are into an area of creative investigation instead of mere reproduction."

Then in 1967 Mike Leigh got a job as an assistant director in Peter Hall's last Stratford season:

"I did some improvisations with the cast of *Coriolanus* and *The Taming of the Shrew* and got treated with a kind of healthy cynicism which was very good for me: I spent the season alternately stroppy and very excited—I seemed to be the only non-Cambridge director around, and I carried my lack of 'A level' English like a great inferiority complex. Still, I did some demonstrations called *The Actor at Work* and then Terry Hands was called away and I sort of inherited *Theatregoround* for a while: but it soon became pretty obvious that the long rehearsal periods I need and the fact that I'm unable to offer managements any sort of a script before the first night ruled me out of most company's schedules.

"So I went off into the wilderness for a while, taught in the E15 acting school, then spent a year at teacher training college in Manchester because I thought maybe I was going to be a playwright after all, in which case teaching would have paid the rent. But there I began to do some improvisations with the Youth Theatre and that sort of led me back to stage work."

An Interview with Mike Leigh

CLIVE HODGSON/1979

M IKE L EIGH MADE HIS only film for the cinema, *Bleak Moments*, in 1971. Since then, he has divided his time between the theatre and television, with a string of successful stage productions, and four feature-length films for the BBC. He scored a major critical success in both media in 1977 with *Abigail's Party*, first at the Hampstead Theatre, and later as a BBC *Play for Today*. Leigh recently completed his first-ever radio play for Radio 3's "Drama Now," and he is currently at work on a new play for the Hampstead Theatre. Like all of his work, it is being developed without a script, through workshop improvisations with the cast.

The NFT season will include all of Leigh's work on film, but not, regrettably, his three productions on video tape: *The Permissive Society* and *Knock for Knock* (two half-hour plays for the "Second City Firsts" series), and the television production of *Abigail's Party*, though the BBC will be rectifying this shortcoming to some extent by repeating the latter to coincide with the season. Leigh is already established as a major figure in contemporary British drama; this unique opportunity to see his films will hopefully establish his equal (if not greater) status as a filmmaker.

MIKE LEIGH: My first television film, *Hard Labour*, produced by Tony Garnett, was made in 1972, and went out the following year. Then about

From *Film* (75:9), July 1979. © 1979 *Film*. Reprinted by permission.

two years went by before I could get any more work in television. The
things I've done since then—apart from work in the theatre—are *The
Permissive Society* (1975), *Nuts in May, Knock for Knock* (both 1976), *Kiss of
Death* (1977) and *Who's Who* (1978). We did *Abigail's Party* for the box, but
it doesn't really translate. Those were all for the BBC; the only thing I've
done for ITV were the titles for *Plays for Britain*. There are also five films in
the can that I made for BBC which have never been shown. It's an idea
that I've had for ages to make self-contained film dramas that only last five
minutes each, so that you turn on the box every day at the same time and
you see one of these things, and they're always completely different—
except that you might have a character surfacing in one film who you've
seen in a different context in another film, or there might be an issue
which cross relates. Five minutes is something that an audience can assim-
ilate in a television context. Indeed, it's a television idea, and a short for
the cinema would *not* be the same thing. It would be fairly pointless if you
only did one film like that, but if they were done regularly over a period of
time, you could begin to create a broader tapestry that would accumulate
into an epic experience. My scheme was to do thirty of these over a long
stretch, all evolved from workshop improvisations and filmed on location.
We did five as a pilot in 1975, which Tony Garnett produced.

What were the films about?
One of them was called *The Birth of the 2001 F.A. Cup Final Goalie,* about a
couple over two years, getting married, debating whether or not to have a
kid, and ending six years later with the husband playing soccer with his
son in a futuristic landscape. All in five minutes! Another of them was
Afternoon, a fairly hard-hitting study of three housewives on the piss in
the afternoon, constructed in such a way that by the end of five minutes
it was very intense. *Probation* was a very straight thing about a black lad
going to see his probation officer for the first time. *Old Chums* was simply
a study of two blokes—one an invalid, and the other something of a brag-
gart—talking about old times on a Sunday afternoon. And one of them
was as trite as you can imagine: it was called *A Light Snack,* and it ran parallel two completely unrelated stories, one about a guy nagging hell out of
another guy in a sausage roll factory, intercut with this thing about a mid-
dleclass lady trying to leave the house just as a window cleaner arrives.
That, in five minutes, is good fun filmically, but in the overall context of

the thing one would be able to look at different aspects of society. The liberating thing from an artistic and filmmaking point of view — the thing that you couldn't do within the context of a single piece — is to actually do all sorts of different things *stylistically*. Hopefully, sometime, that scheme will get off the ground, but meantime they lie fallow in cans.

Would you like to do more work for the cinema?
I'd love to do a fairly large-scale feature film about an air hostess, approached in exactly the same way as my other things. But it would have to be done on a big scale, so there's no point in suggesting it to the BBC. And I would like to make another film that was done very slowly and intensely, like *Bleak Moments.* Although it is possible to do something like that for television, in the end, the shooting *is* very tight — the shooting is set at a certain length before they even know what the film is, so you can't decide how long to spend on things. The difficulty with the cinema is that if people who've got scripts can't get backing for decent films, then I'm *right* out of the race. And although I don't pretend that *Nuts in May* was as fundamental as *Bleak Moments,* it was nevertheless an attempt at a certain kind of piece — more a satire than a dramatic investigation — and had it been a feature film, I'm quite sure it would have taken off. In some respects, it would have been *better* as a feature film. *Abigail's Party* never played to an empty seat at Hampstead, and we had offers from three different managements to go into the West End with it. It *was* commercial and money was made out of it — but with no more than the usual intention on our part to be commercial. Which indicates to me that if one is given the freedom to just get on with things, one can create work that might easily be commercial. If you tried to set-up something like *One Flew Over the Cuckoo's Nest* in this country, you *might* — if you were lucky — get BBC to do it as a *Play for Today.* But you'd never get it off the ground as a feature film.

The Private Hopes of a Prophet of Gloom

HUGH HEBERT/1988

WHEN MIKE LEIGH CHOOSES titles like *High Hopes* for his new film and *Smelling a Rat* for his new play, it's not surprising the whisper was that cheerfulness had finally broken in. He did nothing to discourage that. His programme note for *High Hopes* at the London Film Festival began, "I used to be a complete pessimist, I now realize. I thought life was inherently and inevitably awful." He admitted to being more hopeful. He sees *Smelling a Rat,* which opened at Hampstead Theatre last weekend, as a kind of anti-farce.

What has somewhat grieved Leigh about the generally happy welcome for his Hampstead *Rat* is that some of the old accusations have surfaced again, if only in muted form. One is that he patronizes lower middle class characters, like Vic in the new play. Vic is No. 2 in a privatised pest control company, played more like a Timothy Spall character part than anyone played by Spall ought to be. He reveals verbal pretensions above his supposedly appointed station.

That is not the way Leigh sees him: "Vic is a celebration of a guy who reads a lot of books, has a vocabulary, is an *individual,* enjoys language even if he may get it a bit wrong. If you create a character so idiosyncratic, some people won't engage because the character is not easily placed. So in some quarters he is seen as an affectation, but he's absolutely real." After all, Leigh says he is a cartoonist manqué, he cites Rowlandson, Gillray, Georg Grosz as formative influences in his early days in the graphic arts.

From *The Weekend Guardian,* 17 February 1988. © The Guardian. Reprinted by permission.

And the cartoonist's art is much the same as the old definition of the Fleet Street hack's: simplify, then exaggerate.

If there are any dramatic influences too, and they don't exactly stick out of his pockets, he would cite Beckett and Pinter, and among filmmakers Renoir, Lang, a telling list for the way they hint at his mix of naturalism and heightened realism. Though Leigh is set apart by his now familiar method of building characters with actors up to the point where they have, in effect, a text. And he feels victimized by the attention always paid to the method rather than the meat.

Mention comparisons with Ayckbourn and Leigh's body language, always graphic, becomes explicit if not expletive: he sits right back in the chair. This is a comparison he says he cannot see, even though it often seems clear to other observers. Ayckbourn, he suggests, is "more affable, less concerned with essences."

Yet Leigh's blacker work sometimes feels like Ayckbourn fallen among tragedians; and Ayckbourn begins to feel more like Leigh. Both delve in the same uneasy areas of family and personal relationships, the same crippled forms of communication. In *High Hopes,* Cyril and his sister Valerie have no idea how to relate to their widowed mother. But Cyril can befriend any stray who has lost his way—in this case, a likeable incompetent who keeps turning up again, suitcase in hand. It is Cyril's girlfriend Shirley, warm and comforting as a velvet cushion, who brings son and mother into a kind of communion again. In *High Hopes,* Leigh's characters not only undergo change, that change enhances their lives, at least for a while. Paradoxically, though the film can be seen as moving the political content of Leigh's work a notch higher, the resolution is entirely personal, within the characters.

"In my early plays, you seldom saw change in the characters, it was more a slice of life. But there was the neurotic need not to repeat myself, to move on. In *Bleak Moments* (his last film for the cinema, 17 years ago) it seemed appropriate to deal with what you might call private acts, loneliness, isolation, non-communication, without looking at the society outside. In a crude sense I was being very pessimistic, there was a sense of doom.

"In the early 1960s, when I came down to drama school in London (from Salford), it was entirely respectable for artists of any kind to say, 'I'm apolitical.' The only politics we got engaged in was CND. By the end of the Sixties, there'd been a shift. I would find it very difficult now not to see my characters in the broader context, because one's much more concerned with the way things are. And being a parent now—sons, 11 and 7—I'm also concerned with all those relationships, parents with children, men with women. It's not new for me to be interested in a caring society, and in holding on to values, but I just felt the need to have a couple of characters directly concerned with that."

In the past, he has been castigated by the far Left for not showing his working class characters manning the barricades. "But this never concerned me, and it still doesn't. I saw *Meantime* on a couple of occasions, one in Hackney, one in Sydney, when someone got up, in each case from the far Left, and said it was a bourgeois, fascist, reactionary, it didn't show the working class spirit—though they were both jeered at by the rest of the audience.

I've no doubt *High Hopes* will be subjected to the same sort of treatment. But I'm really concerned with stimulating discussion—and entertaining people too. I want people to go away *without* the answers. And that's not a cop-out."

The optimism and the politics may not go that deep, and they are not as new in his work as some suggest—maybe we should have, say, *Bleak Moments* revived on stage by a different director who sees it as a true comedy that just happens to have a couple of tragic victims thrown in.

The comedy is far broader in these latest pieces, and the touch—in *High Hopes* anyway—much lighter. The laughter rolling round the NFT at the festival showing confirmed that change from his recent television films. *Meantime* (Channel 4, 1984) is about a family marooned high in a crumbling tower block, father and two sons all unemployed and gnawing at each other. It observes the corrosive power of unemployment, it is political in its picture of enforced dependency that only outside agencies have the power to ease, if none to cure. But as in *High Hopes,* the more optimistic resolution—and it *is* there—is in the reconciliation between the warring brothers.

Home Sweet Home, made the previous year for the BBC, does not even offer that marginal relief. It rummages in the lives and grubby linen of a group of postmen and their wives, men without job satisfaction, women without man satisfaction, children issued to the wrong parents and one girl turned inwards by neglect and a string of social workers, each rubbishing the previous one's theories.

Four Days in July (BBC) was about Northern Ireland, and might have been the noisiest and most political of the lot.

Yet it works marvelously and quietly at a humanistic level, even though you may distrust its symmetry—the parallel lives of two couples, Catholic and Protestant, awaiting their firstborn.

Leigh says: "A great deal can be conveyed to an audience about the way the world might be, by showing the way the world is." It is a naive article of faith these days, but sometimes it works and the operative word is "might," not "should."

The Leigh Way

ROBERT GORE-LANGTON/1988

MIKE LEIGH IS 45. After twenty years in the business as a
writer/director he is now known as a champion of the improvised play.
No, no, you can hear him say, weary of the battle to undermine the con-
notations of the word—scriptless happenings, unfocused direction,
embarrassed actors and the rest. Leigh would argue that, on the contrary,
finesse has always been his aim. His subject matter may not obviously
reflect his cultural interests accumulated through an extensive education
during the Sixties at RADA, art school and film school. In terms of content, *Abigail's Party* or *Goose-Pimples* don't leap to mind as being the work
of a man absorbed as a student in the film work of Renoir or Ray, the art of
Georg Gross, the German Expressionists, or the theatre of Pinter, Beckett
and, above all, Peter Brook.

The improvisational aspect of his work is rooted in a commitment to a
personal theatre aesthetic. Leigh has undoubtedly had an influence on
other director/devisers—Mike Bradwell of Hull Trux, for example—and
on student drama, too. Over the years he has worked on the Fringe ("I did
plays that nobody ever saw," he recalls with a smile) and with school and
student drama, working with E15 Acting School and the Manchester Youth
Theatre. His first real piece as a "deviser" was with Peter Hall and the RSC
at the Other Place, producing *Babies Grow Old* there in 1974. Since then
there have been innumerable films and theatre pieces, the *Silent Majority*
being his first major stage landmark.

From *Plays and Players*, November/December 1988. Reprinted by permission.

His return to the stage after seven years of filmmaking is an event of some note. The play due to open in early December, at the time of our interview, had no title and since the play, in his customary manner, is being manufactured during the rehearsal process, Mr. Leigh was guarded about its content. (All I can say is that this play is being done over Christmas and the new year and that it won't be completely free of laughs), was the full extent of his revelations. A Mike Leigh panto, perhaps?

His work—and there's been a good deal of it—has always been rooted in a commitment to both stage and screen. His passion for both is realised in a double dose this year, with *High Hopes,* a new feature film shortly to be released and another play scheduled for "creation" in Sydney next summer. Since *Goose-Pimples,* his last stage work and his first West End transfer, there have been four films. *High Hopes* is his first feature since *Bleak Moments* in 1971, which characteristically was evolved out of the stage play for the Open Space. "I'm passionate about film but in the end theatre and film are functions of the same thing," he says, keen to stress the importance of the one to the other.

Indeed, a preview tape of the forthcoming *High Hopes* displays all the characteristics of the Mike Leigh stamp. It's a look at the New Britain writ small—stage size in fact—in the domestic world of a group of Kings Cross inhabitants. Bearded Cyril and Shirl are the weary socialists with a cactus called Thatcher (because it's a pain in the arse), their decrepit mum-in-law, a couple of yuppie immigrants, the miserably vacuous sister Val and her disgusting, rich husband. While the characterisation verges between farcical exaggeration—the Sloanes twosome are as gruesome a Leigh creation as you will find—there is in the Marxist couple's idealism, long since outflanked by circumstances and reality, a touching portrait of a resilient love.

This latest work he feels connects directly with his professional roots. "My earliest so-called improvised plays in the mid-Sixties were structurally like film. Crudely speaking, I became more committed to sustained dramatic action. The better I got at dramatic action in the theatre the more it paid off in film. I do regard both as mutually beneficial." This current production for Hampstead is not a theatre addicts "fix" after years of abstinence, more a redress of a few years imbalance. "There are things about the theatre which you cannot help but love—mainly to do with the living performance and all that. But equally with film it's a wheeze to get things seen.

"We calculated that when *Goose-Pimples* closed at the Garrick that 35,000 people had seen it. That's peanuts compared with the millions who saw *Abigail's Party* in the TV version, which went out when it was raining, with an ITV strike, something boring on BBC 2 and before Channel 4 was invented."

The whole question of the watershed success of *Abigail's Party* (it continues in more or less continual performance via French's acting edition) is not without its sourer note. His empathy with his characters is mistaken for disgust. "I'm not given to whining about critics but I resent that brand of criticism which runs 'these Hampstead *Guardian* readers are sneering at working class values etc.' These plays are not about 'them' but 'us.' They're a lamentation not a celebration. The biggest tragedy for me was that *Ecstasy,* which many thought to be the best thing I'd done and in itself a deeply serious statement, was written off—in the most extraordinarily ignorant way—as a superficial sneer at the working class."

With *High Hopes'* rejuvenating humanism, Leigh may well be staking out fresh territory: the cast which includes Tim Spall, Saskia Reeves and Brid Brennan—"young actors who are prepared to go out and bring back material to the rehearsal room"—certainly bodes well. Leigh would like to think so, he remarks, before scuttling back to his beloved rehearsal room.

A Conversation with Mike Leigh and Alison Steadman

JUDY BLOCH/1991

JUDY BLOCH: *Your film titles have evolved from* Bleak Moments *and* Hard Labour, *through* High Hopes, *to* Life Is Sweet *and its Regret Rien cafe. Does this represent an evolution in your thinking about how people are able to cope, live their lives? Are people doing better? Or is it something personal?*

MIKE LEIGH: I think it's unconscious, in a sense, and probably more personal; I certainly don't think it's a reflection on the way people are living their lives, which hasn't gotten any better, really. On the contrary, it seems a bit worse. But the suggestion, that you are not necessarily making but that some people have, that I've gotten more optimistic leaves me feeling pretty uncomfortable, because I think that's simplistic. I mean if you look at the earlier stuff, the general tendency is to say, by implication, that life could be better, and that's really what *Life Is Sweet* boils down to.

[But] *Bleak Moments* and *Hard Labour* were made by a person in his late twenties; and *High Hopes* and *Life Is Sweet* were made by a person in his late forties, nay a middle-aged person. In a very personal way, some of my things are plainly pre-parent and some are post-parent. [Leigh and Alison Steadman have two children.] And as you get older, life, or everything, is in one sense a lot more complex, a lot less black-and-white, and the later films I think have a greater complexity, for that reason.

This is the complete text of an interview excerpted differently in both *The University Art Museum and Pacific Film Archive Calendar* and *Film Quarterly*. © 1992 by The Regents of the University of California. Reprinted from *Film Quarterly*, Vol. 45, No. 3, Issue: Spring 1992, pp. 52-53, by permission.

JB: *One of your themes seems to be that our society makes it difficult, if not impossible, to be grown up. The young couple in* Grown-Ups, *the childlike wife in* Nuts in May, *the father who can't father in* Home Sweet Home... *And perhaps the parents in* Life Is Sweet *whose childlike behavior elicits all kinds of weird adult qualities in their children...*

ML: I think you're right, I think the job of actually making the journey from being a child to being a real grown-up is a pretty tough one, I'm not too sure that I've accomplished it.

ALISON STEADMAN: No, you haven't...

ML: But I think it's very interesting in a way—and this is not necessarily something that I've actually dealt with, as such, yet: We grew up at a time in the forties and fifties when kids were kids and grown-ups were grown-ups in many cultural ways. And that is eroded in some respects, in a way that's not necessarily helpful. And again, the whole question of how society organizes itself in terms of people really having responsibility for their own lives, having control over their own lives, as opposed to being, as it were, looked after by the mother state, poses all kinds of questions about how we live and about democracy, about one kind of political system or another. Those are some of the questions that are on the agenda in *High Hopes,* for example. And what I do is, to a great extent, have the antennae out or, if you like to mix metaphors, take the temperature of the time that we're in... And [this] certainly has to do with the way most people, ordinary people in the world, have to get on with the business of coping with the entirely disorganized and irrational business of living. So we were indeed just kids left to it.

JB: *Representatives of the supporting structure, that which is* supposed *to be supporting us, for instance social welfare workers, are represented in the films as infantilizing and moralizing.*

ML: Yes and indeed... especially in the earlier films, [there are authority figures] who are reactionary and intolerant, which traces back to some figures of authority in my own life. He said daftly.

JB: *The parents in* Life Is Sweet *seem incredibly immature, yet Alison's character, in particular, pulls off this wonderful rescue of her daughter, surprising, coming from that character who was still trapped in her own childhood.*

AS: I don't know whether I'd entirely agree that Wendy is immature herself, only because, although on the surface she appears to be quite lighthearted, and perhaps a bit silly and a bit frivolous, she's not one-dimensional. There are several sides to her, so that as the film unfolds, you see that, beneath all of this, she is the rock of the family, and the guiding light.

M L :   I'm aware that one of the prevailing themes or issues in all of the films is the hopelessness of being truthfully what we are as opposed to what other people expect—what our received roles are. And that does manifest itself all the way from the central character in *Hard Labour*— whose problem is that she's confused about what other people expect of her—right through to *Life Is Sweet,* which contains characters like Nicola, like Aubrey, who are receptacles of received notions of how they should be; right through to Wendy's final [dialogue, which says] we can just talk about it, be honest and we can really get somewhere.

And that obtains right down the line in every single film. Though, for example, if you take a character like June in *Home Sweet Home,* there's no *discussion* about what I'm talking about, except that she's so encrusted with frustration about the reality of her own life that she oscillates between escaping into a fantasy world of pulp fiction or of being completely unloving towards her partner and all the things that go with that.

J B :   *It seems that in lieu of a plot climax you have a moment when that character does realize who or what he or she really is, sort of a degree-zero realization . . .*

M L :   I think that began to happen later. I think that, in the earlier films, *Hard Labour, Nuts in May,* they don't really face up to who they are . . . *The Kiss of Death . . .*

J B :   *That was one I was thinking of . . .*

M L :   You're right. *The Kiss of Death,* for which I have quite a soft spot . . . was a lot more radical, ahead of the other films for quite a while, because in fact, there *are* elements of coming to terms with things, facing up to things and questions, and it anticipates *Meantime* and *High Hopes* (by more than a decade in the case of *High Hopes*).

J B :   *That one line, at the end, when his friend apologizes to him and he says, "It wasn't you" . . .*

M L :   That's right. And that film is really about what we're talking about. It also contains one of the few absolutely genuinely all-improvised scenes — there are hardly any—but one of the key scenes in that film *is* improvised, because it was done with the little girl, the bridesmaid...I don't think it's the best constructed scene but it's got quite a lot to say in the context of what we're talking about.

JB: *Now that we're on the subject of style and acting, I don't know if you wish to talk about...*
ML: Well, I've never been asked, so therefore, I never have the opportunity to discuss it, so at last, you chanced to mention it...[Laughs] Sorry, this is more than just an interview, this is The Archive.

JB: *I know that you workshop the characters and a little bit about that. My first question is, is it serious business when you're doing it?*
ML: It is very serious, but there are plenty of laughs along the way.
AS: We wouldn't do it if there were no fun involved.
ML: No, there are times when it is an absolute scream, of course, but it is, in the end, serious, and I may say, an extremely grueling and arduous business.
AS: It can be quite tedious as well...The amount of work that's involved, particularly as you get older and your character's older, so you've got more background. It's not so bad when you're only sixteen, you haven't got much to go back on...
ML: To be honest, 20 years ago I found long rehearsals, investigating the relationships, the research, endlessly fascinating, and in some respects I find it something of a chore now. Having said that, what I find ever increasingly delightful and pleasurable is the process of actually filming. Which compared with the rehearsals is chalk and cheese; the rehearsals you can keep, as far as I'm concerned. Whereas filming gets more and more exciting.

JB: *Do you think you may end up writing scripts?*
ML: No, not at all, that's merely an expression of how it is. Couldn't do it, certainly couldn't do it as *well*. [Our process is] partly long-winded because no stone is to be left unturned; you have to investigate everything you can think of, and more, in terms of the characters, their world, their background, everything they've experienced. You know, this is standard procedure: we spent a couple of days during rehearsal for *Life Is Sweet* inventing what happened to them on certain holidays in Spain. Now that's not merely an exercise—not merely to do what we *were* doing on one level, which is to

extend the scope of their experience; not merely to open up something which could possibly earn its keep in the film (which it happened not to); but at the same time, most importantly, it's part of the ongoing thing of spinning their lives and thereby spinning their ongoing *relationships*. So that of course when they were in Spain Nicola disappeared for a whole night and they were wondering what had happened to her, and they got worried. But of course that was before we had got to the actual stage of her condition as it was in the actual picture. And we dealt in some depth with Andy and Wendy's time and background as teenagers. All of those things are entirely necessary.

AS: They pay dividends, ultimately, when you come to actually roll the camera on them as they are now.

ML: But even if you decided to say "let's cut all this," the thing is, you wouldn't, because you don't know where you're going, in script terms. And also, it's part of the job, which is not to be underestimated, of actually creating them so that we really believe they exist.

JB: *That explains a lot about the experience of watching these characters whom you've created: watching, you have to keep reminding yourself that these are actors, and I think that's the way it pays off. But there's sort of a paradox in that kind of intense creation of reality: in the end, in a certain way they're not real, they're super-real characters.*

ML: I think that's right. This revolves around a number of different factors, one of which is, quite simply, what is even the most sophisticated audience's received expectations of how characters in movies behave or are—which is to say, on the whole, not like real people, in behavioral terms. And of course what we're dealing with is making people like people really are, behaviorally. So there's that. Obviously there are considerations involved which have to do with heightening things—which actually are *not* heightening beyond what's real, but because you look at it, you actually start to perceive...As when you're in a subway, right up against someone, you have to look at them, though you try not to, you have to see them, hear them, smell them. That's what it's about, really.

It's also the case that we are in the business of not only making people believe and care and all those things, but *laugh*; we are in the business of being funny, basically, of being comedians and that's not to be underestimated.

JB: *Right, because I get the feeling that there's a certain point at which you're saying to the viewer, "Wait a minute, this isn't life, this is art, you'd better understand that." For me that's the point when a character goes off into caricature.*

ML: I don't believe that I am ever saying to the audience, "This is not life it is art." If that seems to be the case, then I think it is flawed, frankly.

JB: *Well then I could rephrase it: What is going on for you when things take a turn that becomes so extreme, for instance, when the women at the end of Home Sweet Home turn into animals, virtually, with their vicious name-calling . . . ?*

ML: The point is, that is what *happens* to people. All that happens in that scene is that they are behaving like some people behave in certain circumstances. The only way I can really explain anything, in any of the films, is in terms of a real world going on, real life. I mean, obviously I can talk about it on another level, about the aesthetics, the literary style, the shooting style, the choice of visual elements, the juxtaposition of comic moments and all of that, but that's not the same thing, I don't think . . . maybe it is what you're talking about. But in terms of the integrity of what's going on, however high the temperature might go . . . One of the classics is *Grown-Ups*, where they all go absolutely, totally ape-shit—but, with all due respect, you've been in domestic situations where people scream at each other like that; I refuse to believe that you haven't; I know you have. And that's the bottom line. Full stop.

JB: *Where do you find actors who will take on the responsibility of creating a character, with a past?*

ML: It's certainly the case that, in England or Britain, or Ireland, there are huge numbers of very talented actors around. It's partly that there is a great tradition of acting—extraordinary in such a philistine country that there should be a great tradition of anything creative but there is. And I also think that, certainly of actors of our generation and younger, actors who have a real creative urge and also a sense of society as opposed to what people want in [actors—] matinee idols or decorative—I think it's become very prevalent. Actually when I first started doing it, even as late as *Hard Labour*, it was a real quest, I saw about 600 people, literally, to find Liz Smith and Clifford Kershaw, who played the parents, Mrs. Thornley and Jim . . . As time has gone on, and we've got older, there are many many more actors who are able to do it.

Perhaps, Alison, you could talk about your training, because when I trained as an actor-writer, about 1966, that was extremely sterile, extremely uncreative, never did any improvisation or anything; it was really the worst aspects of English boulevard theater acting, or Shakespeare, the old-fashioned mold . . . Less than half a decade later you were training [and it was] very very different indeed.

A S : Yes, the change came in the middle sixties, when the drama school I went to was very progressive for its time. A lot of the work was based on the teachings of Stanislavsky, we did a lot of improvisation, a lot of emphasis was placed on the objectives of the characters, what the characters wanted, and the truth behind [this] . . . To believe in the character, building a character was part of his teaching. So there was less emphasis on the glamorous star, presenting yourself and speaking nicely and looking glamorous, and more on the truth, investigating each play and the background of the characters and all that. Although the improvisation was nothing like Mike does—it wasn't handled terribly well and it kind of ended up as more a test of your ability to just get up and perform rather than any investigation into characters or situations. Nevertheless it was a step in the right direction. But nobody works quite like Mike. I've worked with other directors who use improvisation or who do devised films out of improvisation but it's quite different than working with Mike.

J B : *Are you doing a lot of other work?*
A S : I've been acting for twenty-odd years; the majority of my work is with scripts: I do radio, I do theater, I do television, and films, but I love working with Mike and working in that way.

J B : *When you say "devised and directed by . . ."*
M L : I think one of the biggest single mistakes of my career was to use that phrase and I wish to hell I had always put "Written and Directed by" earlier than I did. For various historical reasons, I thought because I didn't sit in a room and write it, it was better to say "Devised and Directed." Eventually I realized that this is the biggest single red herring of all . . .

J B : *Anyway, I was thinking that if you have a conception of something you want to make a film about, you obviously have a conception of the characters . . .*

M L : The real point is this: all these questions arise in relation to other ways of working, which has to do with writing [a script] in a room and somebody interpreting it. The real truth is that this is a medium in its own right, it's a plastic medium; everything I do that's worth talking about happens in conjunction with the actors. Obviously I make decisions, I have ideas of who the character's going to be, but then it's different than what happens...I create the characters and the actors create the characterizations, but even that is complicated, because I spend a lot of time working with the actors on their characterizations. There are characteristics that people have got that are derived from things that I have suggested or that have come to me from other sources that I've experienced. And similarly there are all sorts of things that happen in the idea of the character that come from things the actors do or say or contribute. So it really is indivisible. I think all of these questions in a way, generally, arise in relation to other modes of operation which on the whole are ultimately irrelevant.

J B : *How has your television work been received by the viewing public? Do people appreciate these portraits of their lives or not...Have you had positive reactions?*
M L : I would say so. I've slightly lost touch, tragically, really, because when they were on television, there was a sort of ongoing constituency that enjoyed them, but because they now aren't seen in that mode—and it's so much harder to get to see [them] because of the perverse distribution system so screwed up by Hollywood—it's harder for me to be quite clear about that. But on the whole it's positive. Except for the minority of middle-class dissenters who always accuse me of being patronizing toward working-class characters, which I completely reject.

J B : *This is not a complaint you receive from working-class people?*
M L : No. Absolutely not. Never heard of it.

J B : *Do you have a working-class background?*
M L : My father was a doctor and I grew up in a very working-class area so the answer is, strictly, no, but yes in many ways because I went to working-class schools and have actually lived in working-class territories throughout my entire life. And I'm married to somebody who comes from

a lower-middle-class background, so I've always had an ongoing relationship with the very ordinary and prosaic world.

J B : *Have you ever had a chance to show your work on American television, PBS?*

M L : No, I think it's a shame. I don't know if that will happen as a result of these retrospectives.

A S : When we did *Abigail's Party* we had to change all the music because of the copyright — we had Elvis — and we were told that if it was going to get sold to the States there would be great difficulties, so we changed all the music to British artists. But it never got sold to the States. And it was very upsetting to have to change all the music.

M L : Subsequent to that, when we did *Home Sweet Home* and all that Sinatra stuff, I said, "You'll have to come on the set and stop me." ... *Abigail's Party* was a bastardized version of the play because of that ... As you know we used Sinatra [singing "I Did It My Way"] in *Home Sweet Home* which means technically they wouldn't be able to show it on NBC or CBS because they would have such an enormous bill ...

J B : *There's an enormous Anglophile population here and they import all sorts of British television, but it's all the mythical British, as in Masterpiece Theater, it's not real. I'd be very curious to see if that could happen.*

M L : These kinds of retrospectives astonish me because I'm otherwise resigned that my stuff is consigned to obscurity, so it surprises me when San Francisco changes the rules.

J B : *I've seen you compared to the following stunning and disparate array of directors: Cassavetes, Ozu, Olmi and Forman. Do any of these stick for you? Is there someone with whom you would connect your work?*

M L : If you'd said Resnais or Nicholas Roeg, I would have walked out and slammed the door, but none of those are that outrageous. I think the comparison with Cassavetes has more to do with a foreknowledge about something that I do with actors than what the actors do on the screen; indeed, what happens to the actors is in many ways pretty different, not only in result but in principle. Not least because this is about actors extending beyond themselves to play characters who are not them, but who are socially placed, character-acting ... And the role of humor is different.

I like Olmi a lot. When *Bleak Moments* came out, some reviewers said it was obviously an homage to Olmi. But strangely, up until that time I'd never seen an Olmi picture, although I was very well educated in international cinema. I did subsequently get to see them all pretty quickly, as soon as I was accused of being influenced by Olmi. And I realized, of course, I'd been very deeply influenced by Olmi. [Laughs] But I understand why that was said.

Ozu is a definite influence, as is Renoir, and Satyajit Ray, and some others. As for Milos Forman: not an influence but definitely an inspiration — in the sixties, when *Blonde in Love* and *Firemen's Ball* were being made, that was a great inspiration to our generation of hopeful filmmakers.

Mike Leigh

JUDY STONE/1991

A s   a   b o y,   M i k e   Leigh drew caricatures until his parents stopped him because they thought he was making fun of people.

The stubbornly individualistic British filmmaker still stirs uneasiness in some middle-class folks who worry that he's being "patronizing" toward the working-class characters in his black comedies.

"The funny thing is that the films are actually about us [middle-class], not about them. Even when we were portraying upper-class people in *High Hopes,* we were still dealing with humanity," Leigh said at the Toronto Festival of Festivals, which was presenting the North American premiere of *Life Is Sweet,* his new comedy about a droll lower-middle-class family in a suburb of London. *New York Times* critic Vincent Canby wrote that Leigh's "gently cockeyed movies are so rich with character that they seem beyond ordinary invention."

Life Is Sweet features an amiable, lazy father who is a professional cook and his wife, Wendy, whose giddy giggle masks a tender perception of their twin daughters' problems. Nicola is an irritable layabout with anorexia, who usually wears a T-shirt proclaiming "Bollox to the poll tax" and has an odd taste for chocolate when involved in her grouchy sexual diversions. Her discreet sister wears men's shirts, works as a plumber and dreams of traveling.

The monotony of their existence is briefly interrupted when a goofy friend opens a French restaurant, the Regret Rien, specializing in such deli-

From the *San Francisco Chronicle,* 21 November 1991. © 1991 San Francisco Chronicle. Reprinted by permission.

cacies as prune quiche, boiled bacon consomme and tongue in a rhubarb hollandaise sauce. The one recipe that's not a delirious invention is a classic medieval dish: a dumpling called "pork cyst."

"I put it in because it's the only one that sounds very silly indeed," Leigh explained. "Of course, the film is a takeoff on nouvelle cuisine. What we're really spoofing is the English suburban restaurant. They're quite desperate—in the British use of the word, meaning disastrous. Awful. Pretentious and gastronomically horrible. But I haven't been to a restaurant as interesting as ours."

For a man whose films are so gleefully offbeat and funny, the short, bearded Leigh seems an almost stern model of sober propriety. That appearance doesn't totally conceal his sharp-eyed marvel at all the wonderful quirks of real men and women. "In a sense I am a caricaturist," Leigh admits. "And I say that without apologizing."

Leigh's goal is "to put characters on the screen like real people: idiosyncratic, unique and individual and properly placed in their social context. Not to do characters like you get in many films. Bland. Real people are by definition interesting. I can sit in an airport or bus station for as long as I have to and I don't get bored because my job is to put that on screen. It involves processes of detail and heightening and distillation. That is in the nature of caricature in the best sense."

For Leigh, the gastronomical spoof is of secondary importance in *Life Is Sweet*. "The primary thing is that as parents you don't entirely get what you think you deserve, and kids don't turn out the way you expect. The parents are quite generous people and in the middle of it, there's a horrible attack of introspection and resentment and that's what it's all about."

Leigh and his wife, Alison Steadman, who stars as Wendy, have two sons, ages thirteen and ten. "At the moment," says their mum with a laugh that's a mere tinkling shadow of Wendy's high-pitched whinny, "I think they would prefer it if I were in *Naked Gun 2½*."

As a girl, she got into training as a comic by "being a clown at home and a clown in school." Growing up in Liverpool, she loved sitting in at the Cavern Club, where the Beatles got their start. "Paul McCartney was everybody's favorite," she said. "We thought John Lennon was a bit surly and aloof and we never dreamed they'd become famous."

She met Leigh when he directed some other students in a London drama school production and felt "a terrific rapport" with his ideas about acting and, especially, his sense of humor. They met again four years later. He saw her in a play in Liverpool and invited her to appear as a finicky, lower-middle-class housewife in *Hard Labour,* his first TV film. Four months later they were married.

The way he works is like "planting a seed," she said. The story comes out of the characters he creates together with his actors in a three-month rehearsal period.

"The thing is to develop the whole world of the characters and that's done not in theory but in practice," Leigh says. "I don't do it in my head or on paper. There's a lot of discussion about the characters. We create and live through years and years of their experiences. There's a lot of improvisation, most of which has nothing to do with what winds up on the screen. One moves forward without necessarily knowing where we're going."

The important thing for Leigh "is that it has the poetry of character. We use a real person as a jumping-off point. I always get the actors to talk about different people they have known. Then, the character develops and expands. My job is to push and pull it and cajole it and bully it in the direction of what's dramatic and cinematic."

At the end of that time, Leigh writes a scenario of three or four pages. It's worked up and written to a very precise state. Then it's shot.

That cooperative way of working partially derives from his experience in Zionist youth groups in the '50s. Born in 1943, Leigh grew up in a gray working-class area in the twin industrial cities of Manchester and Salford, and went to neighborhood schools.

When his father, a physician, got out of the army, Leigh recalls, "There was a Labour government which started a national health service that is now being destroyed by the Tories. The first thing my father did was to dispose of his private patients as soon as he could. He was an interesting combination, in many ways very Jewish but also very Lancashire: direct and blunt. We weren't Orthodox, but there were a lot of Zionists in the family that went back an unusually long way."

The real appeal of Leigh's youth group was that they all went camping. "We shared our money and learned about socialism. We did all that because we were on the production line to become kibbutznicks. It liberated us from the bourgeois, provincial Jewish constraints. We were actually rather anarchic, but we also worked by getting people together in groups and working creatively."

Leigh's immersion into those two different worlds provided him with an unusual perspective. "It finally contributed to my ability to be sympathetic to everybody and at the same time be comic and tragic."

There was certainly a tragi-comic aspect to the scene that erupted when Leigh took *High Hopes* to Krakow, Poland, as part of a British Film Week that took place during that country's first free elections.

A marvelous sardonic slice of British life in Thatcher England, the movie focuses on three couples from different social worlds: the wealthy snobs, Rupert and Laetitia; the newly rich slobs, Martin and Valerie; and the aging hippies, Cyril and Shirley, who still care about other people. Leigh didn't have a clue as to how the Poles would react to the film.

"I was smugly sitting in the back of the auditorium as one does, expecting questions about the budget and the shooting time. But the audience went berserk because this is a film that celebrates socialism, and the heroes are holding on to their values, and they actually go to Highgate cemetery and pay homage at Karl Marx's grave and castigate materialism.

"There was a riot more or less [among the Polish filmgoers] . . . It was midwinter and the public transport stopped at midnight, but they were still in there slugging it out over *High Hopes* with each other as well as with me. It was all quite devastating and confusing and at the same time, sort of liberating, too."

The Director's Improvised Reality

PETER BRUNETTE/1991

"FAMILIES [SCREW] YOU UP," complains a character in Mike
Leigh's 1988 film *High Hopes*. That's still the case in his new comedy *Life Is
Sweet*, opening today, but now Leigh seems to be telling us that families
just might be responsible for many of the good things in life too.

Though this is his 16th film—all of which, according to the British
director, concern "ongoing things like living, dying, surviving, working
and food"—Leigh was unknown in the United States before the release of
High Hopes. Despite that film's success, however, he admits that many of
its anti-Thatcher barbs were lost on Americans.

Life Is Sweet will perhaps be more immediately appealing because of the
universality of its realistic, yet ultimately joyful, portrayal of working-class
family life besieged by teenage rebellion—played for laughs, basically, yet
not without a strong dollop of seriousness having to do with one twin
daughter's bulimia. Here familial squabbling seems normal, even healthy,
rather than something to be fixed, and the parents remain human and fal-
lible rather than trying to be Super Mum and Dad.

Leigh spoke to a visitor recently at the Toronto Festival of Festivals,
where his film had been warmly greeted the previous night. The 48-year-
old director, whose short stature, beard and rounded contours make him
seem slightly gnomelike, was still basking in the afterglow. In a voice
whose dynamic range—from whisper to near-shout—gives evidence of
his early training as an actor at the Royal Academy of Dramatic Arts, he

From *The Washington Post*, 27 December 1991. Reprinted by permission of the author.

distinguished between "real people" and "people in movies," and attributed the natural feel of his films to "not having to reduce everything to a formula even before you start being creative."

For Leigh, Hollywood-dominated films, particularly those about family life, "are kind of dopey, and are just a lot of ciphers and generalizations, stereotypes." Leigh himself refuses to make judgments about his characters. "One of the conventions of classic Hollywood filmmaking is that there are goodies and baddies, but in my films, you don't really have goodies and baddies. Everybody gets a fair crack at the whip. So from [rebellious daughter] Nicola's point of view her parents *are* oppressive, and from their point of view, she's just plain silly. I just try to make the film work, as it progresses, the way you relate to people in real life. You meet someone and you make some assumptions, then as you start to get to know them, the whole picture changes."

Above all, what makes a Mike Leigh picture different is that the filmmaking process is a truly collaborative effort between the director and the cast. The film is created during a three-month rehearsal period and nine weeks of shooting. After all that, "an actor's able to go into character pretty thoroughly and deliver the goods. You want it to feel like it's always been there, and by the time we get to shoot it, it bloody well feels like it has."

So much so, in fact, that one of Leigh's biggest worries is that audiences think the actors aren't acting at all. "These people aren't playing themselves, they're creating characterizations. I cast in a very empirical, instinctive way, partly because I work with people who are known to be highly versatile character actors. Gradually we begin to bring into existence, really, the whole world of the characters. We invented Andy and Wendy [the parents], and we investigated their relationship, and she got pregnant and had twins, and so on. I really don't know where it's going. My job is to be inventing it, and as I do so, I begin to discover, to create the premise for the film.

But all of this is only preparatory, and the real meat and bones of the thing is what happens when the shoot starts. I write a structure that is very brief, like three pages. Scene 1: Wendy at dancing class. Scene 2: Wendy goes home. And each scene is built and rehearsed on location and built up through lots of discussion and very thorough rehearsal until it's ready, and then it gets shot."

Even though there's no script at this point, does he at least know where the story is going? "Yes and no—this is really the most elusive thing of all.

Yes, certainly, a substantial part of it. But I also keep my options open, and invariably, I really don't know how it's going to end. This is normal in dramatic writing: Anybody can do the end; it's getting the beginning and the middle set up that's the problem. If you've got everything else going in the right direction, then the end is there like a harvest to be plundered.

"Obviously, I've got all kind of *ideas* about it, but I don't have to commit myself. Also, the actors don't actually know what I'm up to. In fact, the actors never know anything more about the whole thing than their characters do. For example, the actors playing Wendy and Andy didn't know about Nicola's chocolate-gorging until they came to the screening for the cast and crew. That's important, because it means that you really preserve those tensions and get the reality of the thing."

This sense of a preexisting reality motivates everything Leigh does. "Whenever I occasionally teach film, what I say to student directors is that . . . we should aspire to the condition of documentary. By which I mean that when you shoot documentary, you do not question that the world you're pointing a camera at actually exists in three dimensions and that it would exist whether you filmed it or not. And if we can aspire to that condition with what the actors are doing, so that it really is in three dimensions, and really does go around corners, then the bit that we actually see, the tip of the iceberg, is going to have that solidity to it."

Lest he be thought over-theoretical, Leigh quickly adds: "But I'm quite simply also in the business of entertaining. I mean it *is* art, and I'm pretty serious about that—I spent a lot of time in art school, and I look at painting all the time, I read a lot of books and all the rest of it—but when the chips are down, it is also about show biz and entertainment, and I'm not embarrassed about that, I enjoy that. I enjoy a good laugh, and we take our humor seriously in the sense that we work pretty hard on the gags and the timing, and all that stuff."

Given the unconventional nature of this process, it is amazing that Leigh can find anyone to bankroll his films, and he knows it. "I don't discuss the film beforehand with the producers because they'll interfere too much. And if you ask me then how the hell do you get the money, the answer is that oftentimes we don't."

If *Life Is Sweet* is successful, says Leigh, "ordinary rational folk would presume that would make it easier to make the next one, but I'm afraid I've been around too long, and I'll believe it when I see it. The problem is the long shadow of Hollywood. Apart from the fact that I would accept money from *anybody*, provided there were no strings attached, you'll not find me going to Hollywood, I can tell you that. But you can't just lock yourself away and say you're not going to have anything to do with it. It crops up all the time. It's just completely obvious that we are the colony, we're taken for granted. All the major [American] studios have offices in London, and we all go and see them and they all wax lyrical because they're in the territory and they know there are Mike Leigh films, but it's all a lot of hot air, it's never going to happen."

For this film, the studios suggested Bob Hoskins and Meryl Streep, because of her ability to do an English accent. "Then they said, 'We don't know if anyone's told you this, but Robert De Niro's very interested in doing an English picture.'" Leigh laughs at such suggestions.

Back in the old days, he says, most British directors could aspire only to make TV films for the BBC, and even though they spent all their time "complaining and whining," they now look back at that period with nostalgia. "You never had to think about anything but the film you wanted to make, and nobody ever genuflected over their shoulder to Hollywood. But now you're talking about films having to make money, and you have to think about the only market in the world where it's going to make any money. You can't make money with a film in the U.K. because the only thing people can get to see there is *Terminator 2*. So whether you like it or not — and I don't — Hollywood is there interfering . . . all the time."

Leigh tells a story about a complaint he heard at a recent U.S. film festival that no one could understand what the actors in *High Hopes* were saying. A member of the audience asked why these films couldn't be made more with the U.S. market in mind. "'Look,' I said, 'this is an ethnic, foreign-language, Third World movie from a small island off the French coast. And if you couldn't understand it, that's why. If you understood it a bit, through some cultural overlap, then that's a bonus.' Being committed to making indigenous film — and I don't make films that are exclusively or idiosyncratically English, the subject matter of my films is not English, but universal — you've got to be able to operate uninhibitedly, organically.

"I'm sort of optimistic, though. I hold on to the credo, with one or two others, that if you don't give in, you don't sell out and compromise, you've got half a chance. But the minute you say, well, let's just do this one, like David Puttnam with *Memphis Belle*, which he only made to get the money to do something else, fair enough, but he made it, he made a film, and for me making a film is a big slice out of your existence, and the film exists forever."

Leigh's only worry concerning his film's reception in the United States is whether American audiences will in fact be able to understand his characters' Cockney accent, but he thinks that actually using subtitles (as in the recent Ken Loach film *Riff-Raff*) would be counterproductive. "You're buggered if you give in here," he insists. "If you want to celebrate people and their particular culture, then you have to enjoy their dialect too. My own kids use a lot of West Indian dialect words in their speech, and I love all that and want to celebrate it. So bloody what if they don't get it in America?"

In a Class of His Own

MICHAEL COVENEY/1993

MIKE LEIGH, OBE. HARDLY anyone noticed that one of the few genuinely creative geniuses of contemporary British theatre and film had been honoured in the Queen's birthday list last month. Richard Attenborough (Life Peer), Thora Hird (Dame), David Jason (OBE), Bob Monkhouse (MBE) and Michael Aspel (MBE) were all widely acknowledged in the tabloids and broadsheets. But just before lunch in Muswell Hill, north London, on the day after the announcement of the Queen's list, Leigh's wife Alison Steadman, the brilliant actress who remains best known as the monstrous Beverly in Leigh's *Abigail's Party* (1977), said that the telephone had "not stopped" ringing. It hadn't even started.

The winner of the Best Director prize at this year's Cannes film festival for *Naked*, which opens here in the autumn, is accustomed to being ignored. It goes with the improvised territory. It made a very welcome change, he says, to wander along the Croisette in Cannes and be accosted by total strangers who had seen his film shouting *"Magnifique!"* This does not often happen when he goes shopping in Wood Green or Crouch End.

Steadman had just completed the first week's rehearsal for her next performance at Hampstead Theatre in a new American play, *Marvin's Room*. The couple's teenage sons, Toby and Leo, were hanging around. Leigh himself was in purdah, contemplating his current three-month rehearsal project at Joan Littlewood's old stomping ground, the Theatre Royal, Stratford East.

A couple of weeks earlier, just after he had started work on his first original theatre piece in Britain for five years, Leigh was his usual cheerful self. "I have to say that at this stage it seems entirely unfeasible that a play will ever occur." As usual at this point, Leigh has no script and no idea what the end result will be, though there will be live music, and a cast of mixed race. The theatre can only announce a Mike Leigh play, running for three months from 20 September, and there are no details of anything else in the advance publicity, apart from the names of the actors; they include the Cockney aggressor Kathy Burke, the amazing, rabbit-toothed Ruth Sheen (of Leigh's *High Hopes*), pert and pretty Wendy Nottingham and gifted black actor Gary McDonald.

Mike Leigh fully expects never to be employed by the Royal National Theatre, though its former administrator, David Aukin, is a longstanding admirer who initiated five Hampstead Theatre plays, including *Abigail's Party* (whose fans re-enact "Abigail's parties" all over the world, in the manner of *Rocky Horror Show* reunions). Aukin, now Head of Drama at Channel Four, co-produced Leigh's latest feature film, *Naked*. Since *Bleak Moments,* his breakthrough film in 1971, Leigh has made *High Hopes* (1988) and *Life Is Sweet* (1990) as well as a series of films with the BBC and a handful of stage plays, which are remarkable in the first place for the quality of acting by an incredible roster of leading young performers: Steadman, Pam Ferris, Brenda Blethyn, Anne Raitt, Lesley Manville, Lindsay Duncan, Claire Skinner, Jane Horrocks, Gary Oldman, Tim Roth, Eric Richard, Stephen Rea, Phil Daniels, Philip Davis, Jim Broadbent and countless others.

They are also remarkable for their consistency of texture, lacerating treatment of pomposity and underpinning sense of social justice. Because Leigh is renowned as an improviser and deviser, it is sometimes assumed that his work is random and undisciplined. Nothing could be further from the truth.

Naked opens here in the autumn, around the same time as the play in Stratford. Its success at Cannes means that Leigh can expect to raise more money for his next film. And that, too, will be devised and improvised in rehearsal, directed and edited and finally written in exactly the same collaborative way. The OBE citation listed Leigh as "writer and director," a job description he admits he took a long time to claim unapologetically. "I do not sit in a room and write dialogue. The actors and I script it together and I sit on it. What I write out, half way through the rehearsal process, is the structure. We never know what is going to happen once all the balls have started rolling. But that is the same with all the creative arts, whether we're talking plays, films, or painting. Improvisation is endemic to all of them. I just take that process much further, collaborating on it with the people who will finally perform it. That seems to me to be sensible."

Leigh, now 50, is a small, hunched and watchful creature, the son of a doctor, with a clear and musical Salford accent. His work has been as much misunderstood as it has been praised over the years. This is partly to do with the unique improvisatory style he has pioneered. Confusion also arises in the merciless comic world he invents: is it condescending caricature or blissfully heightened reality when a fat slob played by Timothy Spall in *Life Is Sweet,* on opening his Enfield restaurant, the "Regret Rien (Tres Exclusive)," runs through the proposed menu of triple soufflé, king prawn in jam sauce, prune quiche, saveloy on a bed of lychees and liver in lager? At a recent retrospective of his films at the National Film Theatre, a woman in the audience accused him of cruelty in the depiction of an adulterous housewife shaking out her orange fake fibre doormat as if somehow Leigh was betraying people who never really existed. Leigh defended himself thus: "You may judge it to be cruel, for you are colluding in this film. We gave her what the character requires. It's just who she is. The carpet, like all of my props, was not made but was bought from a shop. So there are plenty of people who have them. Hazel's one of them. If you think that's cruel, that's your opinion but not necessarily mine."

Characters whose speech and mannerisms are grotesque, funny or downright nerdish have led other critics to accuse Leigh of class snobbery or class contempt. But the world of Leigh's plays and films is so heated and intense, the language so sparse, or deliberately ornate in many passages, that the ordinariness of his characters' lives is transformed into something mythical, resonant, disturbing. Leigh's characters are always offering a "nice little cup of tea," or suggesting they "pop the Beaujolais in the fridge," or claiming to have seen "Keith Chegwin in W. H. Smith's," or ordering someone to "stop standing on the rug; you're squashing it," or hoping they don't have "a kid that's a bit thick." These scripts—compendious deposits of exaggerated lower-middle and working class conversational argot—are orchestrated by Leigh into a final, brutally edited story.

Naked is a watershed film—and not just because it has sharpened Leigh's international profile. The subject matter is a mixture of sexual violence, domestic instability and homelessness. It is an epic chronicle which is also Leigh's most potent attempt so far to allow the odyssey of one character to control the film's dynamic. Johnny, played by the gangly David Thewlis (voted Best Actor at Cannes), last seen licking chocolate spread off the bulimic Jane Horrocks in *Life Is Sweet,* comes to London from Salford. In one of his many sexual and philosophical encounters, he tells a girl he picks up in a café, who is house-sitting for classicists, that he is not "Homer-phobic." Their shared tenderness is quickly displaced by violent disaffection.

The emotional volatility of the film is reflected in some very tough physical action: heterosexual buggery, sado-masochism, street violence, all manner of harshness, deception and disillusion. As a vision of life in our big cities it is rivetingly bleak, plausible, exaggerated and hilarious, all at the same time. In a long scene with a security guard called Brian, played with resigned torpor by Peter Wight and shot in greenish neon and a spooky silhouette, Johnny invokes the spirit of apocalypse, pointing out that "wormwood" as quoted in the Book of Revelations translated into Russian as "Chernobyl": "The end of the world is nigh, Bri."

Ten years ago, when he was the subject of an *Arena* profile, Leigh talked about his sense of "outsiderism" as a doctor's son living above the surgery in Salford in the middle of an Irish working-class neighbourhood. His friend, the playwright, Mike Stott rang up to say that he always assumed that the "outsiderism" came from his being Jewish. Some of it does, but Leigh is clearly an outsider by temperament. His paternal grandfather, called Liebermann, came to England in 1902 from Russia. He had been to art school near Moscow and was due to travel on to New York, but missed his connection from Hull to Liverpool and stayed in Manchester. He worked as a portrait miniaturist, colouring in the backgrounds to family photographs and framing them. Leigh's maternal grandfather was a kosher butcher from Lithuania who worked in Finsbury Park, north London. And one of his grandmothers, also Russian, grew up in Blackburn. His parents met in the Zionist youth movement, the Habonim, and Leigh himself was an active member until his late teens. It was here that he began to direct plays and to extend his gifts for clowning and cartooning which he had displayed at the local primary and Salford Grammar schools. At 17, he won a scholarship to RADA and walked away from Zionist culture.

"I had begun to realize that what really fascinated me was the movies. And I wanted to get out of Manchester; the city was not the exciting mecca of anarchy and culture that it is today. I had been reading theatre magazines for years and of course we all went to the Hallé Concerts and to see Gilbert and Sullivan. To this day I remain a closet Savoyard; I play G&S records when I'm on the rowing machine at home." The rowing machine is a recent acquisition, Leigh being mindful of his family history of heart disease. His father, who died eight years ago aged 71, lived a lot longer than his uncles. Leigh has had three hernia operations and lately shed a good deal of weight. "I'm still a lazy fat slob, really, under this very svelte exterior."

Simon Channing-Williams, who has produced Leigh's last three films and formed Thin Man Productions (suitably enough) with the director, says that Leigh does not really leave himself much time for relaxing. "He reads voraciously and is a complete cinephile. He does enjoy a drink or two after a day's shooting, if he is not going straight off, as he usually is, to carry on rehearsing with the actors."

Alison Steadman has always found it difficult to persuade him to take holidays, but she did succeed five years ago and booked the family on a sand and sea vacation—the very idea is anathema to Leigh—in Sardinia. As if that were not enough to put up with, he found yours truly, complete with wife, son and mother-in-law, standing in the same check-in queue at Gatwick Airport. We were all on the same flight, in the same resort, and the same hotel.

I therefore approach each new Leigh film fearing it might contain one of Leigh's more pimply actors as a curmudgeonly theatre critic in less than state-of-the-art leisure wear. Leigh does not swim or play tennis, but he stood around patiently on the beach while everyone else did, and occasionally paddled up to his waist if that was the only way he could find of pursuing a torrential conversation about his own work or that of others such as Simon Gray or Alan Ayckbourn. At least he proved a dab hand at the beach barbecues, which he supervised with deftness and civility.

For there is a dark side to Leigh, the price you pay for his obsessiveness and absorption in his work. He not only remembers every single detail about everyone else's films, he seems to live continuously in the celluloid reality of every one of his own. Any journalist asking a question is likely to have his or her head bitten off with a withering riposte beginning: "I would have thought it was obvious that . . ."

He is given to black moods and long periods of depression, though Simon Channing-Williams says that the stability of his current team, especially his designer Alison Chitty, provides the back-up to see him through the worst days. And most of the actors he works with always want to repeat the experience. Ginette Chalmers, the agent of both Stephen Rea and Jane Horrocks, says that both her clients feel that way. Horrocks, in fact, joined Leigh on *Life Is Sweet* rather than wait on the virtual certainty of making *The Fisher King* with Robin Williams.

In London in the early 1960s, Leigh devoured Peter Brook's experimental work at the Royal Shakespeare Company, and the films of innovators like Renoir, Satyajit Ray, Wajda and Ozu. Another deep impression was made by John Cassavetes's improvised first film, *Shadows*. After RADA, he studied theatre design at the Central School of Arts and Crafts, and filmmaking at the London Film School. So the Leigh method was not something he just hit upon. It evolved from years of study, experience, apprenticeship. And by the end of the 1960s he was improvising plays in Birmingham, Manchester, at the RSC and at the acting school attached to the Theatre Royal, Stratford East. It was here that he met Alison Steadman. He suggested they have a chat, but forgot about it and she went off to work in repertory theatres. They met again once Leigh had got his foothold in the BBC.

Steadman first appears in *Hard Labour* (1973), as the house-proud wife of a car mechanic played by Bernard Hill. Laying out her salads and coleslaws, she declares that what she likes about the estate of mind-numbing uniformity is that every house on it "is just a little bit different." The film's central character, a Catholic cleaning lady played by Liz Smith, oscillates between the old Salford back-to-backs and the stuck-up Jewish household which employs her. There is a mild form of background exorcism here for Leigh, but the real narrative rub exists, as the title suggests, between conditions of employment and issues of child bearing. Liz tells her daughter that she must suffer to bring children into the world, while an abortion is arranged by an Asian taxi-driver played by Ben Kingsley.

One of Leigh's regular actors, Philip Davis, says that David Thewlis is still reeling after the excitement of Cannes, saying that nothing in his life will ever again be as good as working with Leigh on *Naked*. Davis himself is a playwright, a good one, who would never claim co-authorship of any of Leigh's scripts. "It's not a democratic process. All you ever concentrate on is your own character. The rest is all down to him." He says that when you are developing your character in public on the streets, Leigh will sometimes lurk "like an invisible garden gnome if he knows you are going into a particular pub, where he will pop up leaning on the bar, keeping an eye out. Some English actors are a bit snooty about all this kind of thing. But the work is not only extremely hard and worthwhile, there is nothing else like it."

Actors find their characters in the first place by discussing with Leigh, on a one-to-one basis, people they know, or know about. This forms a springboard, or a solid base, for the character Leigh develops with them. On films, actors are never allowed to see their rushes. And nothing is ever shot in a studio, with the exception of *Abigail's Party* which was quickly set up at the BBC because Alison Steadman had become pregnant and could not transfer with the play, as planned, into the West End.

"My job as a dramatist," said Leigh during the NFT Festival, "is to make the improvisation go in the most useful direction. And I look at all my films in the context of the others I have done. I like actors who have a social sense, and a sense of humour, and who are character actors. I don't work with stars, not because I am against stars, but because they usually do not want to work in the way I do. Fair enough."

And what does Alison Steadman think about her husband as he enters another period of anxiety, creating a new play from scratch? "There's delight and there's terror. I'm proud of his commitment, but it's always been tough." If Leigh had compromised his ideas, "We could easily have had a lot more money." Instead there's the acknowledgement of his peers at Cannes and a mounting chorus of approval for *Naked* all over Europe. And the OBE. Had he thought of declining the honour? "Not on your life." Was he chuffed? "You bet."

Mike Leigh Calls It as He Sees It

DAVID STERRITT/1993

BY ANY MEASURE, MIKE Leigh has emerged as the most important English filmmaker of his generation.

From prizewinning satires like *Bleak Moments* and *Meantime* to international successes like *High Hopes* and *Life Is Sweet,* his films have earned praise around the world for their sympathetic yet tough-minded portraits of working-class British life. Feminist critics have taken a special interest in them, noting Mr. Leigh's close attention to the problems of women.

Leigh's working methods are as unusual as the subjects of his stories. He works closely with his cast, developing themes and situations through extended improvisations before the cameras roll. Although the credits may say "Written and Directed by Mike Leigh," each of his films is the result of joint exploration.

Leigh's career hit another high point at the Cannes Film Festival last May, where he was honored as best director for *Naked,* the story of an abrasive and sometimes violent young man named Johnny who barges through a working-class London neighborhood having aggressive encounters with friends, acquaintances, and strangers. David Thewlis, who plays Johnny, also won the Cannes award for best actor.

Developed through Leigh's improvisatory techniques, the film sparked controversy at Cannes with its searing depiction of physical and psychological torment inflicted on female characters. Many critics defended the

From *The Christian Science Monitor,* 7 September 1993. © 1993 The Christian Science Monitor. Reprinted by permission.

movie, however, pointing out that the brutal behavior it depicts is never justified or romanticized.

Mr. Thewlis is the first to agree that the character he plays is "abhorrent" in many respects. "But we didn't put anything in the film to be titillating for the sake of it," he told me at Cannes, where we had several conversations. "We brought a sense of responsibility to everything we did, and fortunately, women seem to understand why they're represented in the film as they are.

"We're not in the business of misogyny or sensationalism," he continued with emphasis. "The scenes of violence in the film are there to make a comment about the society we live in—the inequality between the sexes, the races, the classes. It's all there for a reason."

Asked about the film's abrasive qualities, Leigh responds in a similar way. "*Life* is abrasive for a lot of people," he told me in an interview, "and there's no getting round it. I think a function of art—and the cinema not least—is to confront these things.... I'm absolutely committed as a filmmaker to be entertaining and to amuse; but I am also concerned to confront, as I did in *Life Is Sweet* and other films."

Leigh and Thewlis both acknowledge that Johnny is an extremely bright and educated young man as well as a nasty and dysfunctional one. Thewlis says it was a major challenge to blend the character's loathsome and laudable qualities into a single characterization.

"I've worked with Mike before in less substantial parts," he told me. "But this was such a complex and multifaceted character—such an intelligent and bitter character—that it was difficult to improvise with such speed and vocabulary and articulateness. I remember my brain being on fire, raging with ideas, because I also researched an enormous amount.

"It was a process of putting an awful lot of learning together and coming up with the philosophy and attitude of the character—who became indignant and arrogant, with a sense of superiority for being more informed and enlightened than anyone around him.... And that's how I felt at the time. I felt I could confound and out-argue anybody."

Like many elements of the film, Johnny's intelligence is stressed not to make him attractive, but to make a serious point. "I know university graduates who have no prospects," Leigh says of England, where unemployment is a persistent problem. "They're a generation of people who have been displaced.... I think more people are very intelligent than the [powerful individuals] who run the world realize. But for a lot of those people, it's wasted. They have the luggage of intelligence and education, and nowhere to use it."

Under such circumstances, Leigh continues, people turn to vapid and materialistic pursuits to distract themselves.

"[In the film] Johnny says people have had the universe explained to them, and now they're bored," Leigh says. "As long as something bleeps and flashes at them, that's all they want. I feel disgusted at all that. . . . I hope in some way the film approximates this tension between the spiritual and the material. . . . We privileged people have this extraordinary capacity to convince ourselves that our lives—the momentary business of mankind, like the Cannes Film Festival—is incredibly important. I felt it was time to raise this in the context of the fact that what occupies *most* people is where their next meal is coming from!"

With its mixture of sociological horror and intellectual humor, Leigh's movie could be a hard sell when it arrives in American theaters (courtesy of Fine Line Pictures, its U.S. distributor) after more appearances at film festivals. Leigh doesn't think it will prove too daunting for general audiences, though.

"In a way, the references are incidental," he says, speaking of the wide range of learning that Johnny displays. "They will resonate with people for whom they have meaning, but unlike Peter Greenaway or someone like that, I don't make films to be decoded by intellectuals. I am not a manufacturer of esoteric formulas. I am an emotional and intuitive filmmaker."

It's the Movie of the Decade.
No No, It's Just a Decadent Movie

DESSON HOWE/1994

MOST MOVIES—PARTICULARLY AMERICAN ones—come at you with their turning points and climaxes precharted, and heroes and villains clearly delineated. But British director Mike Leigh, whose films spring out of a unique method of improvisational collaboration with his actors, eschews such predictability. In his internationally known works, such as the already controversial *Naked,* which opened here Friday, *Life Is Sweet* and *High Hopes,* events seem to unfold of their own accord. The effect is a fusion of post-"kitchen sink" realism and good old well-timed comedy, a quasi-documentary satire full of lively Albion archetypes, from yuppie gentrifiers to bike-riding proto-Marxists. Leigh's characters seem to have more *elbow room* to air their idiosyncrasies than others. The possibilities before them seem as unpredictable and serendipitous as life.

Leigh emerges from the elevator in an Upper West Side hotel with an almost weightless gait. He's small in stature, so slight you imagine dust mites could ride the tops of his shoes untroubled as he walks. Only the gray flecks in his beard betray his 50 years. He has been called gnomelike, but he's more attractive and humanly appealing than that.

At a modish eatery not far from the hotel that features roller-skating waitresses, Leigh, who stands at the forefront of a critically acclaimed group of British-based directors that includes Derek Jarman, Terence Davies and Peter Medak, hunkers down for a highly varied menu of Leigh subjects and concerns, without much ado.

From *The Washington Post,* 30 January 1994. © 1994 The Washington Post. Reprinted by permission.

"My ongoing preoccupation," says Leigh, establishing his credo, "is with families, relationships, parents, children, sex, work, surviving, being born and dying. I'm totally intuitive, emotional, subjective, empirical, instinctive. I'm not an intellectual filmmaker. Primarily my films are a response to the way people are, the way things are as I experience them. In a way, they are acts of taking the temperature."

If so, *Naked* is the most likely to crack the glass. In an era when sexual roles have become so acutely examined, this modern allegory full of disturbingly rapacious encounters drew fire at Cannes, where Leigh nevertheless took the director's prize—and David Thewlis the actor's award.

In *Naked*, hyper-intelligent drifter Johnny (Thewlis) has a genius-level knowledge of Western philosophy and theology, but he's an illiterate in his dealings with women. As soon as he seduces them (and with his loquacious, witty personality, he's extremely successful), he turns verbally savage and physically abusive. As Thewlis—in a separate telephone interview—describes Johnny, "He has grown up with a distaste for sex. So he blames women for his own sexual arousal."

Far worse than Johnny is Jeremy (Greg Cruttwell), a loathsome landlord who bullies women into sex, treating them throughout with misogynistic disdain. "I hope I didn't give you AIDS," he says to one such conquest, by way of pleasant, postcoital talk.

How much the women participate in their victimization has been the main bone of contention. Leigh is angry at those who have concluded that, by portraying a misogynist, the film actually *is* misogynistic. He points approvingly to two critics, Georgia Brown and Amy Taubin of the *Village Voice*, who have reviewed the movie with unequivocal enthusiasm. The *Village Voice*, in fact, hailed *Naked* as "the movie (quite possibly) of the decade."

Leigh considers their reaction "the serious, mature feminist position—that I'm delighted with—that has no problems with the film at all. There's another kind of reaction, which is annoyed by the film because it shows women being weak—"Why aren't the women shown more positively?"— all that stuff. To be honest, I feel that's kind of naive. The film plainly is neither pornographic, nor is it a celebration of male dominance...."

"I would also question how much rape there actually is in the film. I would argue that, whilst in no way, obviously, does one condone any kind of rape, every situation that's shown is of people who are there by choice for whatever sad reasons."

Leigh speaks with an almost professorial indignation, like a hip college teacher amazed at the wrong-headed interpretations of his students. To questions that bother him, he takes exasperated, indirect exception. ("With respect," he says to one, "this is confused.")

To the obviously irksome (and oft-heard) criticism that some of his characters (the hoity-toity ones) are caricatures, Leigh points to the restaurant window's panoramic view of the street.

"If you look out the window for a couple of minutes," he says, "you will see idiosyncratic behavior manifest in everybody. Some people will be more extraordinary—or heightened, as it were—in their behavioral characteristics than others. If you then put on the screen [those] behavioral characteristics absolutely accurately, some people will seem more outrageous than others. That's what gives rise to this [critical] nonsense."

He cites a waitress who, a few minutes before, had lost her footing and landed in a heap behind the director. If he were making a film about this interview, he says, he would include the fall "because it was there. But people would read it as a patronizing attitude toward the waitress. Actually, it happened because it happened."

At that moment, there is a crash of cutlery behind him from a neighboring table—an almighty din. Leigh inclines his head toward the noise and says, "See?"

Leigh remembers a "happy and sad" childhood in Salford, Lancashire, near Manchester, in the late 1940s, "where you would have eight or nine flick houses within walking distance." His first movie was *Pinocchio,* but as a child he was raised on a diet of Michael Powell, John Ford, Billy Wilder and Preston Sturges. However, at some point in his moviegoing youth, Leigh remembers thinking: "It would be great if we could have people in films like people *really are.*"

His parents were middle-class Jews (his father was a doctor) in a working-class neighborhood, so Leigh, who went to "very working-class schools," moved between two social classes. In 1960, as a "17-year-old little fat boy," he passed up college (to his parents' horror) for a scholarship at the Royal Academy of Dramatic Arts. Although he learned a lot, he says, "we never actually investigated anything real from life. It was all about churning out received ideas of performance."

He studied theater design, went to art school and attended the London Film School. He had a brief, unsatisfying period with the Royal Shakespeare

Company, a minor career as a bit actor, and tried writing in the mid-1960s. But, he says, "I really didn't get a buzz out of the solitary nature of writing. I was fascinated by directing. I wanted to make films, that was clear."

In 1965, when Leigh became an associate director at the Midlands Art Centre in Birmingham, he began working improvisationally with teenage actors. After further refinement in drama workshops and experimental theater, Leigh honed a directorial style in which he gave performers free rein (within his guidelines). When he embarked on his filmmaking career in the early 1970s, he brought the method with him. It has served him for nearly 30 years.

In his films, Leigh casts his actors with only a general sense of the characters they will play — or the story they'll be in. In extensive one-on-one conversations with his performers, those characters are further defined. Leigh then makes the actors (who very often have not met each other yet) interact in small improvisational encounters. During this period of fine-tuning, readjustment and open-ended experimentation — which lasts for up to four months — scenes are completely worked out. Then the script is "written" and the crew invited to embark on the latest Mike Leigh film.

His first film, the 1971 *Bleak Moments* (financed by Albert Finney), about a woman who has to look after a mentally impaired sister, won the Golden Hugo at the Chicago Film Festival. In 1972, he made *Hard Labour* (a downbeat working-class drama featuring a young Ben Kingsley as an Indian cab driver) for the BBC when "the British film industry was alive and well and hiding out in television." The next 10 years was Leigh's formative period, what he calls a "brilliant, fantastic" time in which he made his dramas with no questions asked and a firm TV airing date. *Labour* also marked his first meeting with actress Alison Steadman, whom he married soon after. A brilliant comedic performer, she has appeared in eight of his works.

Working for the BBC for 10 years, then depending on the support of independent television station Channel 4, Leigh's output in the 1970s and '80s was prodigious. There have been more than 40 works for stage and screen, including the plays *Abigail's Party* (a satire featuring Steadman as a nouveau riche socialite, which also became a television film) and *Smelling a Rat*; and the films *Nuts in May* (a popular television comedy in Britain, in which two urban vegetarians go camping), *Meantime* (another working-class story featuring Gary Oldman and Tim Roth) and, *Who's Who* (one of Leigh's few satiric forays into upper-middle-class life).

In the United States, Leigh first became known for the 1988 *High Hopes,* a marvelously comic indictment of Margaret Thatcher's England, introducing such sign-of-the-times characters as two gentrifying snoots and a leftie who mispronounces Nicaragua. Then came the 1991 *Life Is Sweet* (also featuring Steadman), a group portrait of a lower-middle-class neighborhood featuring—among many others—a sullen adolescent given to bulimic chocolate binges and a portly restaurateur who offers such nauseating delicacies as Tongue in Rhubarb Hollandaise. Leigh's films resonate with bittersweet class observations and ironies. The upper class—when it's featured—doesn't fare too well, which is why he was so baffled last November to receive his Order of the British Empire (OBE), Buckingham Palace's royal seal of approval for commoners.

He recalls his one and only meeting with the queen: "She pinned this thing—a medal—on my lapel. And she said"—Leigh affects a royal falsetto—" 'What exactly do you do?' I said, 'Well, I direct films.' She said, 'It's terribly difficult at the moment, isn't it?' I said, 'Yes *Mah'm,*' and she shook me by the hand which, you are told in advance, means, 'Now leave.' And I did."

"It's very stimulating to work with him," says actor David Thewlis—but it isn't easy. "You work until the early hours of the morning, without any predictability. You're never able to make arrangements in your social life. Sometimes you will be required to wait by the phone—and if an improvisation by other actors requires your character to be brought back, the assistant director will call up. He tells you to warm up, and go to such and such a place. It's a bit like being a fireman."

Thewlis became, in his own words, "real obsessive, hyperactive and frustrated" in the role of Johnny. He spent a year reading the books he thought Johnny would be familiar with, an enormous reading list that included the Koran, the Bible and myriad philosophical works. "To be blunt, I was a right pain in the [expletive] at home. I don't think it's easy living with someone who's working with Mike at that kind of intensity. I don't expect to work that hard for the rest of my life."

During one rehearsal period, Thewlis and a Scottish actor got into a spontaneous in-character scuffle on the street, causing a crowd to gather and, later, a police car to show up. As the oglers increased, Leigh crossed the street and quietly ordered the actors to come out of character. The fight stopped immediately.

"The onlookers must have thought, 'What did the little guy with the beard say?'" says Thewlis. "'He should work with the U.N.'"

Asked about Thewlis's dedication, Leigh says he discourages complete role immersion as "unhealthy." But he acknowledges that his creative process "takes you over. I think I suffer from that too. For six months you don't go out, you don't eat, go to the movies, socialize—[working] 14 hours round the clock, day in, day out."

Time is running out. It's time to settle the bill. The waitress comes back with the change.

"Have a great afternoon, guys," she says.

"We might have a *reasonable* afternoon," says Leigh, after she leaves. "I don't know how great it'll actually be."

Mike Leigh's Grim Optimism

HOWIE MOVSHOVITZ/1994

THE DEMISE OF THE British film industry has been lamented regularly since Alfred Hitchcock came to this country in 1939. It's true that British filmmaking never has been a huge economic force, but there have been good British directors working in Britain all along. Sometimes they leave and come to the U.S.; sometimes they stay home; and sometimes they go back and forth between Hollywood and London.

The pessimism runs so deep, though, that even great British film successes are bemoaned as signs that the industry has fallen into ever more dire straits. And while it's true that money is dreadfully tight for film production, to judge by the films at film festivals over the past few years, British filmmaking looks like a healthy enterprise in creative terms. Peter Greenaway (*Prospero's Books*) has a film at Cannes and Telluride every couple of years; Ken Loach received a tribute at Telluride in September and his film *Raining Stones* is one of the delights of the year.

Lord knows, you wouldn't want to confuse Ireland with Britain, but Jim Sheridan, just nominated as best director for *In the Name of the Father,* which was, in turn, nominated as best picture, is directing and writing actively; and British director Mike Newell (*Enchanted April* and *Into the West,* written by Sheridan) works successfully in both Ireland and England.

Maybe the best of the British filmmakers is Mike Leigh, who was honored at the Denver International Film Festival last October. Along with

From *The Denver Post,* 22 February 1994. © 1994 The Denver Post. Reprinted by permission.

Loach, Leigh has a love and a fascination with the working class, people who've suffered particularly from the social dislocations caused by Thatcherism and whom Leigh sees as struggling to maintain their identity (*Life Is Sweet*), their sense of humor (*High Hopes*) and their sanity (*Naked*).

Naked, Leigh's latest film, opens Friday. I had a chance to speak with him in Cannes last May about the film, in which David Thewlis plays a man so dispossessed that he's become a wanderer and a ranter. The character is brilliant, perhaps, but he has no direction for his intelligence and no perspective on himself. Leigh won the director's prize in Cannes, and Thewlis won the award for best male actor.

Naked is a grim film in some ways. Johnny not only looks lost, he's got a nasty edge that makes him at first quite dislikable. But what comes through, and it's what Leigh looks for most of all, is that the character rings true.

"As you know, I go to considerable lengths to be sure that when we film, we're filming some kind of actual emotion. The tension's really there. But I've tried to construct it to force you to confront your own responses. The way I set Johnny up to start with is in the worst possible light, so that you've got to come to terms with the fact that he's actually a good guy."

Leigh attributes the sense of deeply felt truth of his characters to a unique way of working, an approach that, in Leigh's own terms, seems to contradict the entire history of filmmaking and drama. He doesn't know what he's going to film until it actually happens. The film is created in rehearsals.

"In broad terms," Leigh said in the close, noisy back corner of a Cannes beach restaurant, "I gather a cast together and we go into rehearsal for, in this case, four months. It's a question of creating characters and investigating their relationships, backgrounds and their ideas, and arriving at the premise for the film, and then working from a very simple structural outline.

"I then build the film up on location by rehearsing it from an improvisational state into a very tight, very highly disciplined condition, sequence by sequence, and shoot it. What goes to the cutting room is highly structured and disciplined. It's the kind of work that is obviously highly creative and collaborative for the actors. But the contributions of designers and cameramen are greater than normal because everybody shares all aspects of the work. So you can get a rock-solid inner truth—textural, social accuracy—

and a heightened, distilled cinematic, dramatic even hopefully — although it sounds pretentious — poetic end product."

Leigh says he knows very little at the beginning of a project beyond vague impressions and a sense of what outsiders might call theme.

"I know a lot and nothing at the start. I'm not an intellectual film-maker; I'm an intuitive and emotional filmmaker. So, I have feelings on the go and conceptions, which are more from the gut than the brain."

Leigh said a list of incidentals bears on his planning. He'd been disappointed that the structure of *Life Is Sweet* limited Thewlis to two scenes and he wanted to make a film with Thewlis in a more prominent role. At the same time, as he entered the project that became *Naked*, Leigh wanted to focus on a male character because his two previous movies centered on women.

Beyond these interests, Leigh was thinking about the state of the world, homelessness, poverty and what he called "the tension between spiritual and material values and the sense of impending doom."

"All those things were on the go without me actually knowing what the film was going to be. You don't need to know that. All you really need to know is what you're going to do next."

Even the shooting of a film has this planned-but-not-planned spirit. Leigh seems to have a conceptual framework somewhat in mind, but the specifics wait until everyone joins the process.

"For this particular film, Dick Pope, the cameraman, was around earlier than normal. He and the designer and I sat down and I said, 'I think we're going to do a kind of film that's a kind of journey this guy's going to be on. It's going to be nocturnal and (show) the unacceptable side of urban life.' We started to experiment with a bleach bypass photographic process that gives you a grainy, monochromatic quality.

"We never know exactly what we're going to shoot until it comes to the actual shooting. I don't storyboard the whole film. We work out the shooting in the location. There was a huge amount of conceptual preparation that went on."

If someone who'd never made a film said he was going to take Leigh's approach, you'd think he was crazy — or maybe just irresponsible. The films he's already made, though, prove he knows what he's doing and they show that he's anything but a loose flake drifting through the cinema.

"It's not just four months of sitting around and talking," he said. "All those things are worked on in a hands-on way—about how characters look, how they behave. The actress who played the other sister in *Life Is Sweet* (a plumber) can now fix your toilet.

"Principally, there's a lot of acting that goes on, a lot of improvisation, a lot of work on the character, the behavior, the accent. A lot of investigation of the relationship and going down roads that don't lead directly to what goes on on the screen.

"For me this is the most exciting way of writing. I am a writer, but what I write in my ivory tower with my quill is a lot less interesting that what I can do with actors. The whole convention of writing a detailed script and then finding the right actor to me doesn't make sense. I don't want to throw out the whole history of the movies and theater, but, for me, it doesn't make sense.

"For me, to get the actor in on the ground floor, to draw on the actor's experience, to be able to make the part fit the actor as well, to know that only (that actor) could have played that part, is immensely beneficial."

Naked: English Director Mike Leigh Turns His Uncompromising Vision on the Way Things Are

JAY CARR/1994

YOU NEED ONLY COMPARE the title of Mike Leigh's new film, *Naked,* to his previous two, *High Hopes* and *Life Is Sweet,* to discern the change in direction. Like any self-respecting observer of British society, Leigh decries in his films the hammering of the working class, the stripping of its dignity, the permanence of its unemployment. But while *High Hopes* and *Life Is Sweet* celebrate the resilience and coping abilities of working-class folk, *Naked,* which opens Friday, is much darker, shoving England's dispossessed proles into a life—if you can call it that—where the only self-validation comes from violence.

David Thewlis, the actor playing the protagonist in *Naked,* has been hailed for his corrosive brilliance and vilified for the misogyny some say he embodies as a drifter named Johnny who lurches from Manchester to London, rapes several women and is himself brutalized. Throughout, Leigh refuses to detach Johnny from the human race. He's not even the worst character in *Naked* (a sadistic yuppie landlord is).

Nor should *Naked* be read too closely as an allegory of present-day England, Leigh cautions, warming to his subject, pulling his ankle up under him as he settles into an armchair over tea in a West Side hotel suite. Yes, it was shot at night in a stylized way designed to make London seem apocalyptic. "But it's not about England or about Britain," Leigh says. "Well, it is, but that's not its primary agenda.

From *The Boston Globe,* 27 February 1994. Reprinted courtesy of The Boston Globe.

"The fabric of society is crumbling in England, there are people all around the streets. And while *High Hopes* was on one level a lamentation for socialism being something that maybe has gotten lost somehow, this film, if I come out of the closet about it, takes more of an anarchist view. I despair that society really will be able to organize itself, ever. In the last couple of years, look what has happened in the world. So in that sense the film is about something fundamental rather than just local. In the end, what it is about is this guy, like a kind of lost communication satellite, floating around the atmosphere, wasted. It's about the waste and the unpredictable nature of things, as I see it.

"I mean, I do worry as to where we are going. I wanted to do a millennium film, and the peculiar thing I felt about a possible impending apocalypse is that it doesn't seem incredibly unfeasible now. Although there are plenty of homeless people in England, I didn't want to make a documentary about homelessness. In a sense, I think the film crosses the park of homelessness without actually dealing with it as such. Although everybody in it, in a manner of speaking, is rootless, or at least displaced. So it is about that. So the discussion about family continues, but here by default rather than directly. It would be nice if his energy could be positive. There are moments when he's with someone and shares an idea, where you maybe feel there's some importance in that, what you'd call positive. I think he is a waste, personally."

If Leigh's conversation seems edited as he goes along, it's an extension of the way he makes his films — "devises" is the word he prefers. He and his actors start with only the most skeletal of scripts: "Scene 25. Office block. Johnny meets Brian." From these outlines the characters are developed individually and in ensemble. Leigh and the actors find their way to the characters, which is why riveting behavioral detail is often the real subject of Leigh's films. "Brian," from Scene 25, is a philosophical night watchman in an empty office building, guarding nothing. He and Johnny have a skewed debate before Johnny notices a woman in a window across the street and moves on her. "I know why she was there. She knows why. We invented her whole life. But you don't need to know that. The ambiguity has to do with how I finally render the tip of the iceberg," Leigh says.

Leigh's films aren't expensive by American standards: With a budget of $2.5 million, *Naked* is his extravaganza. That doesn't mean there's any imminent prospect of Leigh signing a Hollywood contract. Hollywood

likes to see scripts, and Leigh never has one until after the improv sessions
with the actors. "It could happen, but it hasn't," Leigh says about a Hollywood deal. "It got very close to it. If it happens, brilliant. If they are
prepared to say, 'Fine, go for it,' and it's genuine—no interference with
subject matter, no interference with casting, final cut, etc., etc., etc.—if we
have it in writing and it's real, great. Otherwise, forget it. I am, after all, a
Third World filmmaker from this obscure island off the French coast. I'm
committed to making indigenous films. I don't want to deviate from my
territory.

"So they say, 'We understand you, we appreciate you, but could you just
give us half a page?' But that half a page can screw up the whole proceed-
ings. If you put it down, you've defined something and you've got to do it,
even if it's not right. I couldn't have given anybody a half-page about
Naked before we did it. There's no getting around it. You cannot compromise on anything so basic and fundamental. To be honest with you, I'm
glad this has only really come into my life at the age of going on 50 now.
I'm glad because I'm too old to be seduced by it. Maybe 10 or 15 years ago,
I would have been. But now I don't care and I am not bothered by it,
really." In other words, Leigh stays independent by keeping the numbers
small and manageable.

And by attracting the cream of British acting talent. Part of the reason
Naked took the shape it did was that Leigh promised Thewlis he would
make it up to him after Thewlis' role as the boyfriend in *Life Is Sweet* was
reduced. After writing plays, Leigh made films for TV before turning to
features. Among the actors eager to work with him: Gary Oldman, Ben
Kingsley, Tim Roth, Julie Walters, Frances Barber, Alfred Molina, Timothy
Spall, Jane Horrocks. Also Alison Steadman, his wife and frequent star,
who won awards for her chirpy matriarch in *Life Is Sweet*.

Leigh takes pains to yank the conversation away from actors to his crew,
whose loyalty and skill he relies upon, he says. Anticipating criticism of
Naked as misogynistic—a view he rejects—Leigh stresses the fact that the
film's crew comprised women as well as men. "We need to have women
there" behind the camera, he says. "It's good for the actresses, it gives a
healthier balance. Also, you feel more comfortable shooting things that
might be more male-dominated because there's a sort of natural sensor.
You're talking about very precise and very creative kinds of work. This
kind of film—vibes are it.

"Beats me how I got it all together," Leigh says, looking back. "My father was a doctor in a mostly working-class neighborhood in Salford, which is a suburb of Manchester. He described my ambitions as 'the moonings of a stage-struck girlie.' Albert Finney and I went to the same school. He backed my first picture, *Bleak Moments*, in 1971. The reality for me — when films appeared in the late '50s like Jack Clayton's *Room at the Top* — was that they fulfilled what I'd felt throughout the decade as an avid, movie-watching kid, which is, 'Why can't people in movies be like real people?' That was the jumping-off point, that's where it comes from. I kind of choose to live in an unfashionable part of London — north London — and my kids go to a state school, and all the rest of it, you know. I worry about the world in which they'll find themselves. But people go getting born every bloody minute."

I Find the Tragicomic Things in Life: An Interview with Mike Leigh

LEE ELLICKSON AND RICHARD PORTON/1994

IN AN ERA WHEN the "death of the author" has been loudly proclaimed, the work of the British writer-director Mike Leigh disproves this kind of facile generalization and suggests a new model of authorship. Perhaps one of the few figures who will eventually be remembered as equally important within the history of both British theater and cinema, Leigh (who trained as an actor at the Royal Academy of Dramatic Art) is known for creating plays and film scenarios that are the product of an intimate process of collaboration with unusually talented casts. Although the only full length study of Leigh's stage and screen work to date is entitled *The Improvised Play*, it is important to emphasize the fact that the actual performances of his plays and the shooting of his films involve no improvisation whatsoever. By the time a fairly lengthy rehearsal period ends, Leigh incorporates the actors' contributions into a final script, and remains as much in control as any traditional director. It is possible to fetishize Leigh's working method, and he appeared to lampoon himself in a 1982 BBC documentary in which the actor David Threlfall played a character named "Mick Leeming."

Most American filmgoers first became aware of Mike Leigh with the release of *High Hopes* in 1988. Nonetheless, anyone who was fortunate enough to be able to attend the Leigh retrospective in 1992 at New York's Museum of Modern Art (featured at several other U.S. venues as well) soon realized that a director who had been touted as a newly discovered talent

From *Cineaste*, v. 20, no. 3, 1994. Reprinted by permission.

had actually made nine feature films, as well as a number of shorts, that predate *High Hopes*. Of course, the primary reason that American audiences were so woefully ignorant of a man who is increasingly being recognized as a major international figure can be attributed to the fact that, with the exception of *Bleak Moments* (1971), all of Leigh's early films were produced by the BBC. The tony Public Broadcasting System, an outlet that was eager to ply Americans with the genteel pleasures of *The Forsyte Saga* and *Upstairs, Downstairs,* was never tempted to broadcast the less soothing but infinitely more challenging Leigh films of the Seventies and Eighties.

Leigh's films have familiarized viewers with a fictional landscape that is instantly recognizable, and, despite superficial and largely misleading resemblances to older British directors such as Ken Loach, sui generis. (Anyone who has spent some time in England has met at least several people who resemble full-blown 'Mike Leigh characters.') With the notable exception of the upper class milieu of *Who's Who* (1979), a Leigh film is usually preoccupied with the alternately grim and comic lives of working class and lower middle class families who find themselves in the midst of crises that are as absurd as they are seemingly insurmountable. *Bleak Moments,* for example, is an almost cruelly funny examination of the preternaturally shy and the sexually inept. Yet Leigh's films are, in the final analysis, not misanthropic, despite the almost ritualistic accusations that his harshest critics fling at him. A fair-minded analysis reveals that he treats his characters with equal amounts of compassion and astringency, a fact that is sometimes obscured by the films' dispassionate tones. Radical audiences have been particularly confused by a left-leaning director who has no inclination to make films that will inspire the working class to mount the barricades.

By the standards of Hollywood narrative cinema, very little happens in a Mike Leigh film. Although Leigh resolutely refuses to engage in sloganeering, his films are acutely political, since they consistently articulate an often hilarious critique of everyday life. This critique is always rooted in the idiosyncrasies of individual characters. To call the films character-driven would almost be an understatement, since Leigh's work is constantly fueled by the sometimes endearing and frequently infuriating eccentricities of quintessentially English individuals. The films are either straightforwardly satirical or coolly empathetic. *Nuts in May* (1976), for example, is a relatively merciless attack on a priggish couple's faddish vegetarianism, while *Kiss of Death* (1977) juxtaposes a sympathetic, if undeniably risible, treatment of an adolescent boy's gauche attempts at romance with an unsparing account of his unglamorous job as an undertaker's assistant. The later films, particularly *High Hopes* and *Life Is Sweet,* are bittersweet indictments of Thatcherism that remain remarkably free of cant. Although *High Hopes'* Cyril and *Life Is Sweet's* Nicola condemn the Tories with frequently articulate fury, Cyril's mixture of cynicism and languor and Nicola's lonely self-loathing prevent these rebels from being the exemplary heroes that some viewers would undoubtedly prefer. These complex roles require exceptional actors, and Leigh's films have benefited enormously from the participation of, among others, Gary Oldman, Stephen Rea, Frances Barber, Jim Broadbent, and the brilliantly malleable visage of Leigh's wife, Alison Steadman.

Leigh's latest film, *Naked* (1993), is similarly irreducible to political or esthetic clichés. The film's protagonist, Johnny (David Thewlis), is neither a hero nor a villain, and ends up being both victim and victimizer. Despite the fact that critics unfailingly refer to Johnny as a "drifter" or "marginal character," this Mancunian adrift in London is decidedly not a "homeless person," but an abrasive loner who consciously rejects the humdrum annoyances of domestic life. Like Dostoyevsky's Underground Man, Johnny celebrates his "own free and unfettered volition . . . inflamed sometimes to the point of madness."

Naked's picaresque, open-ended narrative is dominated by two concerns that occasionally intersect: verbal invention and alienated sexuality. As the film's voluble catalyst, Johnny spews forth monologues of sometimes breathtaking, if crazed, eloquence, and engages in a series of trysts with troubled women who find themselves initially attracted to his torrent of words, but are eventually repelled by his contemptuous abuse. The sex in *Naked* is the complete antithesis of Hollywood's soft-focus coupling— what Nabokov once derided as the "copulation of clichés." In fact, any idea of 'sexual union' is alien to *Naked's* protagonists, since the characters' frantic writhings ultimately accentuate their essential aloneness.

Although some literal-minded viewers have chosen to interpret Leigh's foregrounding of Johnny's frequently unsavory sexual misadventures as an endorsement of his misogyny, *Naked* highlights some of the most noteworthy moments of female solidarity in recent cinematic memory. Toward the end of the film, Louise (Leslie Sharp), Johnny's stoically dejected ex-girlfriend, listens to her chronically discombobulated, if sporadically witty, flat-mate, Sophie (Katrin Cartlidge), bemoan the fact that "men don't like you if you're strong, don't like you if you're weak, hate you if you're clever, hate you if you're stupid."

Naked combines the near anthropological precision of Leigh's previous films with a heightened stylization that makes this film both his most allegorical work, and his least specifically English. Johnny's aimless journey into the depths of London's netherworld allows the film to fortuitously swerve from the ruminations of an oddly metaphysical nightwatchman to the fulminations of a yuppie named Jeremy (Greg Crutwell) who may be the most loathsome character Leigh has ever created. And, at the moment when the film appears to have reached a pessimistic cul-de-sac, Leigh introduces a character named Sandra (Claire Skinner), whose inability to finish a sentence makes her surface fastidiousness thoroughly ridiculous.

Like *Naked,* Leigh's most recent play, *It's a Great Big Shame!* (produced in London during the fall of 1993), is both a radical departure and a work with tangible links to his previous grim farces. *It's a Great Big Shame!* juxtaposes a first act that highlights a Victorian couple's turbulent marriage with a second act that deals with an equally fractious twentieth century black family who live in the same East End neighborhood. The play was both Leigh's first period piece and a scathingly unsentimental attempt to explore a Britain that is no longer racially homogenous.

Cineaste interviewed Leigh last fall after a screening of *Naked* at the New York Film Festival. After the film had opened commercially in New York and London, we called Leigh at home in London to discuss the film's popular and critical reception. Although Leigh is certainly not someone who suffers fools (or foolish questions) gladly, he is a generous, funny, and insightful interviewee. His frequently trenchant observations help to illuminate certain common misconceptions about his work and reveal the surprisingly autobiographical roots of a man who is Britain's most consistently provocative contemporary filmmaker. — **Richard Porton**

CINEASTE: *Do you feel that your films are involved in a politics of inquiry, posing questions rather than providing answers?*
MIKE LEIGH: Absolutely, totally. I don't think they come up with any answers. Interestingly enough, from some people's perspective, that is, people on the far left, my films have come in for quite a lot of hard criti-

cism. For example, *Meantime* and *Hard Labor* were both criticized very severely from the extreme left for wasting the opportunity of propaganda, for not actually coming out clearly with a statement, with answers. Not showing people fighting back, not showing heroes and all of that. Indeed, all of the films—and *Naked* in particular—ask for more questions than give answers. For me, the whole experience of making films is one of discovery. What is important, it seems to me, is that you share questions with the audience, and they have to go away with things to work on. That's not a cop-out. It is my natural, instinctive way of storytelling and sharing ideas, predicaments, feelings, and emotions.

C I N E A S T E : *Don't the criticisms you've cited reflect certain leftists' demands for positive cinematic heroes? Johnny is not a proletarian hero.*
L E I G H : Absolutely. It's ludicrous, and all the negative criticism of *Naked* has been along those lines, whether from the left or so-called feminists. The serious feminists haven't had a problem with it at all. I make no apologies for the fact that I continue to discover what I've been discussing for some time after I've made the film. I can see a film years later and actually realize what I've been dealing with. For me, that's what it's about. These things are multifaceted, and are made from the gut. In the end, these aren't cerebral films.

C I N E A S T E : *Naked does seem to mark a transitional point for you. Even the darker visual style is unlike anything you've done before. The film seems to open up a wide range of possibilities.*
L E I G H : It does. At that level, I wanted very strongly to move away from a domestic perspective.

C I N E A S T E : *In a way, the domestic perspective was very suitable for television. Did the fact that your early films were made for television influence the choice of subject matter?*
L E I G H : Well, to be truthful, I'm very militant in my resistance to that line of thinking. I don't think one thing has anything to do with the other. A film is a film, whether made for the cinema or television. I got a lot of this in England. Even when I made *High Hopes* and *Life Is Sweet,* people said, "Well, he's just making those television films again." I think that's a lot of crap. I don't even think the television films are television-like. I've seen them on big screens and they work.

CINEASTE: *Yes, I agree. I just thought perhaps the subject matter was influenced by the choice of form. Television is meant to go into the home, after all.*
LEIGH: The truth is that, whether we like it or not, people look at movies, epic movies, every day on television. Forgive me, though, if you weren't slighting the television movies. It's something we all get very defensive about.

CINEASTE: *What was the impetus for the apocalyptic tone in* Naked? *Is it related to the state of England today?*
LEIGH: No. You deal with one thing, and then you deal with another. That's what I'm dealing with. One could have made *Naked* several years ago, although I do think things are getting worse. There is a sense of impending doom. I just thought that, after completing several films from a more positive perspective, it was time to do this. Obviously *High Hopes* ends a trilogy of more political films, and it was concerned with, in the end, socialist preoccupations. This is a more anarchist view of the world, and maybe deep down, along with layers of Sixties conditioning, one I feel with more conviction.

CINEASTE: *Unlike Cyril, the protagonist of* High Hopes, *one couldn't imagine Johnny, the working class protagonist of* Naked, *visiting Marx's grave at Highgate cemetery.*
LEIGH: No, absolutely not. He has a different perspective.

CINEASTE: *You're in the Labor Party, aren't you?*
LEIGH: No. I am not connected to anything. That's the whole point about *High Hopes*. I may contribute money to the Labor Party. I am a nonmember of anything.

CINEASTE: *In some respects, all of your work is imbued with an antiauthoritarian, or even anarchist, spirit.*
LEIGH: If my obituary said, "Mike Leigh: Filmmaker and Anarchist Died Yesterday," I would be horrified. I don't primarily regard myself as an anarchist. This issue comes under the category of received politically correct orthodoxy. By instinct, my emotional politics are as much socialist as they are anarchist. In the end, one has deep misgivings about institutions, governments, and humanity's ability to organize itself so that things make

sense and work. That's what I'm talking about. I don't otherwise subscribe to anarchist orthodoxy. We're talking about my gut reactions here.

This strand goes right through my films. You've got it in *Bleak Moments.* You've got it in *Nuts in May*—the dogmatists and the people who are just letting it hang out and getting on with it. The goodies in that film are the guys who are just getting on with it, and the really healthy couple on the motorbike. You've got a strand throughout of people being battened down and trying to fight out in various ways. Obviously this is true in *Meantime,* in reference to Mark, the Phil Daniels character. *High Hopes, Life Is Sweet,* and *Naked* all have disaffected youth.

CINEASTE: *There is frequently a tension between the individual and the collective in your films, isn't there?*
LEIGH: Yes. Apart from that, and it's certainly an ongoing theme, there's the tension between conformity and the individual. The preoccupations in *Naked* are preceded by all sorts of things . . . like *Grown Ups,* the film where you have the authoritarian figure, the teacher, next door.

CINEASTE: *There is a naive assumption on the part of some viewers that they can't like a film if they can't "identify" with a character.*
LEIGH: Some people need that. What we're mostly talking about here is what people feel safe with. People like to know where they are, or they like to persuade themselves that they know where they are. You don't have to know where you are, actually. You go away and discover after a period, by gestation.

CINEASTE: *Perhaps part of the problem is that people expected something else from* Naked. *As Ian Buruma has observed, it's not a film about homelessness or Thatcherism.*
LEIGH: I think that's it. It's partly, of course, that *Naked,* more than any of my films, certainly in the U.K. has had an image created for it, perhaps inadvertently by the press, quite far from what the film actually is. For example, people say that it's quite funny and quite compassionate, but many people have the impression that it's this relentless, humorless, nihilistic bile. Of course, that's not true. Whatever film you watch, assuming you've seen a film before, you immediately go into one program or another, or plug into an expectation system. If the film is any good, these

expectations are constantly confounded. If *Naked* works for anybody, you certainly go through that process.

CINEASTE: *I think many people have participated in an active misreading of the film. There is a struggle for clarity in all of your films which make these misreadings frustrating. And sometimes an almost primal misunderstanding is the very subject of your films, which makes it all the more ironic.*

LEIGH: You're right. In a way, it is ironic. But somewhere in and amongst all that is the extra ironical dimension that if, in the film, A says X to B, B misconstrues X as meaning Y. I don't put in all kinds of semaphores to make sure that unintelligent members of the audience get it. I just put it in there like it is. The irony is that people misunderstand message X, just as B misunderstands message X. In other words, some people are dumb. Of course, it's not as straightforward as that. Is it not the case that people are so encrusted with layers of indirectness, and received prejudices, and received notions of whatever? Again, we're back to PC and all that rubbish.

CINEASTE: *You achieve something interesting by stressing both great intimacy and a clarity through distance.*

LEIGH: That's true. Alienation. My feeling is that—I don't know if it's statistically true of the majority of people—but, for what it's worth, the majority of audiences don't have problems with any of this. They get on with it, because the actual currency of my films is very direct, in real time, and you can understand the parameters of what's going on. But there is this clutter of prejudice. What you're presumably talking about is some kind of semiotics, of what people's language of looking at films is about.

For example, one of the consistent confusions and criticisms—rubbish, really—about my films has to do with caricature and behavioral tics. Part of the actual substance, narrative, thematic—the content of my films—is the detailed study of how people actually behave. In other words, behavioral study. The characterizations are very detailed in terms of actual physical, rhythmic speech patterns—like real people, like you and me. Some people have an odd response to this, because they are used to characters merely being ciphers, and are not used to having people rendered, moment to moment, like real people. The distilled reality of this converts itself into a set of symbols which people become self-conscious about.

They can walk out of the cinema and see people behaving in an equally idiosyncratic way, if not more so, and they wouldn't see it in terms of signs and symbols. They would just see it as people behaving in the way that they behave. Viewers who don't have any problems with my films are just responding to the way people actually behave.

CINEASTE: *Naked seems to have an almost terminal quality. Most of your other films have dealt with families or groups of people. Everyone is very much alone here.*

LEIGH: Yes. It is about displacement—people displaced from their families. I've dealt more with families than just about anybody, but in this film I felt the need to address the situation of people who have drifted away from their families. There have always been people like that.

CINEASTE: *Did this preoccupation with displacement precede your usual close collaboration with the actors?*

LEIGH: That's both complex and straightforward. As a writer and film-maker, I have a number of ongoing preoccupations which inform my casting choices, and how I push the characters as I create them. It's academic, in a way, this business of where it evolves in the rehearsals. On one level, you wonder about the streets of London where people are hanging about. On another level, as a parent, I do wonder what kind of a world my kids will live in when they're my age, or whether this world will even exist. I can't address such things in a film, except by having someone preoccupied by it.

CINEASTE: *The neighborhoods didn't seem readily identifiable, except for Soho. Was this deliberate?*

LEIGH: Yes. This is very important. You do know where you are in *High Hopes* and *Life Is Sweet*. It is very important to stress that this film could be anywhere—New York, Berlin, wherever. It is *a* London. Soho, if I may use the word cautiously, was shot in the most naturalistic mode. We really did shoot in the streets and people walked through the shots. We filmed all night and there were no extras. Some of the locations, such as where Johnny goes and talks about the "bowels of London," are concoctions of wasteland London, that one being near Bricklane Market.

CINEASTE: *It is, then, a film about the breakdown of community and solidarity—both political and personal solidarity.*

LEIGH: Absolutely, and about the crumbling of the edifice.

CINEASTE: *If, then, things are getting worse in England, how do you see them getting worse?*

LEIGH: If we talk about England, in reference to *Naked,* we should do so cautiously, since, as I've said, it's not just about England. However, if we do, the fabric of society is collapsing. People are insecure. There is a sense of disintegration which is, as much as anything else, a legacy of the Tories. But I think this sort of thing is happening everywhere. It's not necessarily a British prerogative. Since the film is, as much as anything else, concerned with a global perspective, I find it difficult to expend too much energy discussing it as a metaphor for the collapse and decay of the United Kingdom. Whereas you could talk about *High Hopes* in those terms. It is important, as well, that *Naked* includes people from different regions.

CINEASTE: *There is perhaps a certain nostalgia for the north of England in* Naked.

LEIGH: I don't think it's a nostalgia for the north exactly. It's a kind of roots, and these are rootless people. Of course, when Johnny asks the Scottish kid, "What's Scotland like?," he says it's "shit."

CINEASTE: *Did you incorporate any personal experiences into the film? Did you observe kids like these on the streets of London?*

LEIGH: Actually, I was hitchhiking from Calais to Paris in 1961 and it was raining heavily, really pissing down, and I fell in with a guy called Wilson McDougall wearing a kilt who came from Paisley outside of Glasgow. This guy—who was completely, totally thick—was trying to get to Paris. Eventually, I had to ditch him in Paris because I was going to Marseilles to catch a boat to go work on a kibbutz. This guy just festered at the back of the cranium for thirty-odd years. I suddenly thought, I could include a bit of him in this lad Archie. There are a lot of Archies around. Johnny has certain personal points of reference as well. Things are quite often autobiographical for me.

CINEASTE: *Is there a conscious doubling of Johnny and Sebastian, AKA Jeremy, the predatory yuppie character?*

LEIGH: Yes, certainly. Johnny is complex and he starts off being very unacceptable indeed. We also learn that in some ways he's very compassionate. It seemed important, in order not to let contemporary male behavior off the hook, to have someone even worse than Johnny, as bad as he sometimes is. They do reflect each other, in that sense.

CINEASTE: *It seems significant that Johnny is speechless after encountering Sebastian. He finally doesn't have a retort.*
LEIGH: That's right, mainly because he's in a rotten condition. We did investigate alternative scenarios, but, in the end, this seemed more apropos. How do you confront a guy like Sebastian? Louise confronts him, but you know he's going to get into his Porsche, bugger off around the corner, and perhaps rape someone else. That's the problem, short of her actually castrating him, and that didn't seem appropriate.

CINEASTE: *And he runs, at the slightest provocation.*
LEIGH: He deals with it by walking away. That's what had to happen, and it seemed important that you not get the direct confrontation you might expect.

CINEASTE: *That would be too melodramatic.*
LEIGH: Yes. Not interesting. Not meaningful.

CINEASTE: *It seems of interest that the women are unusually responsive to characters like Johnny and Sebastian.*
LEIGH: Well, one is inclined to think that, in these postfeminist times, these so-called liberated times, women are not victims. I don't think this is entirely true. I also think it's important to show what happens if you have someone who is aggressive, cheeky, and charismatic. I think of these things, in a certain sense, on a semiotic level, and I use the word semiotic very reluctantly. This has to do with the aspect of moving imagery which you put in a film. Here is a mover—the central character is charismatic. In some ways, he is sexy and intelligent, but he is not the sort of person you usually find in a movie because, in some ways, he is ugly and unacceptable.

CINEASTE: *Isn't this the fascination of the film? You can never pigeonhole Johnny.*

LEIGH: Yes, absolutely. If we take him seriously as a real person, then you have to ask, how do women deal with him? There's one woman who's very strong and copes with him. There's somebody else who is nuts. There are a couple of people who are displaced. And, finally, there's Sandra, who is probably also nuts, but, on the face of it, responsible.

CINEASTE: *Johnny is a character who exploits people's vulnerability.*
LEIGH: Yes, but, apart from anything else, these things are a function of his own vulnerability. I think the naivest interpretation anyone could put on the film is that there is Johnny and everyone else is a victim. He's as much a victim as everybody else, in a certain respect. Of course he is, socially. The fact that he is an outsider to start with is a function of society.

CINEASTE: *The response to* Naked *from women has been very positive, especially from* The Village Voice *critics. As far as we know, the only woman who termed the film misogynist was Claire Monk in* Sight and Sound.
LEIGH: Yes, all the negative reviews have been British.

CINEASTE: *The British seem very hard on their own filmmakers, as opposed to their frequent praise of foreign directors.*
LEIGH: The British are hard on anything British, and films are no exception.

CINEASTE: *I've had the impression that the film was much more enthusiastically received in the States.*
LEIGH: The English response to this film has been very cluttered and confused, full of prejudices. There have been two or three reviews from the States, I can't remember which, that have worried about the women. *The Village Voice* is very on the ball, it seems to me. You cannot meet more respectable feminists than that lot. People who attack the film for being a male, misogynist, sexist indulgence or whatever, overlook one overpowering, salient fact, which is that you do not make a film by yourself in an attic. All filmmaking has to be in some way collaborative, and my filmmaking is more collaborative than any. You don't make a film like *Naked*, with those kind of female roles, and have dumb bimbos playing the parts. The only kind of actresses who you're going to get to do that kind of work are highly intelligent, highly motivated, highly politicized feminists. No

other kind of actresses would be any good at it. And you don't make a film with those kind of actresses without their total commitment and collusion. Not to mention that you don't shoot a film like that without an intelligent crew who wants to shoot it. Insofar as any of this needs to be said.

CINEASTE: *I'm sure that the actresses, in developing their parts, were quite vocal about the film's sexual politics.*
LEIGH: Absolutely. We talked about all of the characters in a very thorough and sympathetic way. We were dealing with the very common predicament of various kinds of women. That's what this film is about, you know.

CINEASTE: *There's a sense of desperation to most of the characters. This seems especially true of the waitress who is initially kind to Johnny. When she finally throws him out, she seems disgusted with her own neediness.*
LEIGH: Yes. Whatever it is she's experienced, she certainly can't deal with it, or confront it.

CINEASTE: *To a certain extent, this character's plight is similar to Sylvia's in* Bleak Moments.
LEIGH: It's funny you should mention that. When *Bleak Moments* was screened in New York some years ago, a young woman stood up and said, "I don't understand this film. I live in New York and I live alone. If I want to talk to people, I just phone them up." I asked if she was absolutely sure. This is ridiculous. There are probably more women like Sylvia in Manhattan than any other place in the world. Of course, the interesting thing is that in *Bleak Moments* nobody says anything to speak of. In *Naked,* they say so much. I'm sure that if Sylvia was more articulate, she would speak to Johnny. She'd get on with Johnny, for sure. Johnny has the bitterness of the Nineties, while the characters in *Bleak Moments* have the innocence of the Sixties and Seventies.

CINEASTE: *You use humor to leaven the bleakness in this film. For example, when Sebastian lunges at Sophie, she rolls her eyes and says, "Here we go again." It's a funny moment, but also a horrible moment.*
LEIGH: Obviously, you know that, of all the characters, she's gotten into these situations endlessly.

CINEASTE: *Is this mixture of humor and grimness something you strive for?*
LEIGH: I don't strive for it. It's something I strive for least. It comes naturally. It's a function of the way I look at life.

CINEASTE: *This kind of gallows humor emerges from the characters, then?*
LEIGH: Yeah. You hew it from the seam, ready-made. I find the tragicomic things in life. That's what the films are about.

CINEASTE: *You seem to devote a fair amount of attention to the books the characters read and carry with them.*
LEIGH: Obviously, Johnny is much influenced by *Chaos*. Both David Thewlis and I were quite taken with it. Once you get into certain areas, it opens the whole thing up. We also got into this whole thing about Nostradamus. Then we discovered this thing about the European bar code. The discovery that the European bar code adds up to 666 was key. We picked that up from a pamphlet. We were walking through Soho, and some nut case offered us this pamphlet. We thought, "Amazing, let's use it." They experimented on the American troops with the laser tatoo. That is definitely a reality.

CINEASTE: *An astonishing thing about your films has always been the use of precise detail. This film is a tour de force in that regard. Johnny's character is a masterpiece of detail.*
LEIGH: It goes without saying that this cannot be achieved without someone like Thewlis. He's an extraordinary actor and an extraordinarily intelligent man. I pushed the boundaries further back, working in this creative way. I've known him for a bit. He was in *Life Is Sweet* and *The Short and the Curlies*. In *Life Is Sweet,* he didn't get a fair slice of the cake. Because of all sorts of developments, I decided that I had to be really ruthless and say, "It does not make sense if you see this guy again." There was a whole thing about him coming back in the end after the accident, and there was a scene with Andy and him in the pub. We shot it, but we had to cut it. He had been shortchanged.

So, when I was getting the next film together, I thought, "Bugger this, I have to get him in. I have to commit myself to him in a way that I don't normally do. He's going to have a disproportionately good role." Once I'd done that, it just set me buzzing in a direction. If ever I fulfilled a promise, it was on this occasion.

CINEASTE: *Claire Skinner's brief turn as Sandra is also a brilliant piece of acting.*

LEIGH: I don't know if it's my favorite scene, but the scene with Sandra gives me such a tickle. Claire Skinner was so successful as Natalie the plumber in *Life Is Sweet,* and I was keen to get her in to do something different. You do the routine thing and check an actor's availability, and, after a while, you make a decision. When we went back, the agent said, "Oh, she's in something else now." It was a television series. But I had to get her in, so I said, "Do this telly series, and you'll have to be a character at the end, and bring up the rear." It was a bonus, because we built up a whole thing about this character. You expect this formidable Florence Nightingale and you get this complete screwball, as nutty as anyone else.

CINEASTE: *You seem to start with the actors, and then other elements accumulate.*

LEIGH: Yes and no. Sometimes these things are a function of economics. You can't afford to have everyone there all at once for the rehearsal period. Indeed, it would be wasteful because people would be hanging about for so much of the time, and I can only work with one person at a time. So I structure it like a pyramid. I started work with David, Katrin Cartlidge, who plays Sophie, and Leslie Sharp, who plays Louise. Then it gradually builds up from there and, within that, you can do all sorts of things.

CINEASTE: *Did you share a close collaboration with Dick Pope, the cinematographer?*

LEIGH: Absolutely, and also with Alison Chitty, the production designer, who worked on *Life Is Sweet* as well.

CINEASTE: *The later films seem much more design conscious.*

LEIGH: The truth is that, despite all we've just said, there are problems with BBC films. They're all shot on 16mm and they're shot very quickly. The cameramen are very good, but the crews are often out shooting documentaries. You can't devote the time to the films and have the same photographic standards that you get with feature films. Roger Pratt, whose work is well known in other contexts, shot *High Hopes.* He also shot *The Fisher King, Brazil,* and *Mona Lisa,* among other things, including *Meantime.* We wanted to spend more time to make something more visually extraordinary.

C I N E A S T E : *The music seems to play an important role in* Naked. *It works especially well with certain long takes.*

L E I G H : It wouldn't be true to say that one thinks about the music as such, although I've never made a film in which there was so much discussion about the music, and so much argument about what kind of music we should have. Of course, you think about the music as you shoot, only in the sense that you think musically, you think of rhythm. That's part of the craft and the conception of the thing, although you're not thinking with a treble clef in front of you. In the end, the music has to go on last.

I usually don't make the decision about who's going to do the music until after we've shot it. The decision here was inevitable, because it was Andrew Dickson, who did the music for *High Hopes.* I think Dickson did a fantastic job, and really challenged every preconception. This is an amazing score.

C I N E A S T E : *Do you feel a kinship with earlier traditions of British cinema?*

L E I G H : I feel an affinity and solidarity with various strands of British filmmaking. We might not necessarily be talking about *Naked* here, but, to some degree, my roots are in Ealing comedy. Certainly these films were on the go when I was growing up — Mackendrick, Hamer, and the whole range of them. I saw a lot of films from an early age — some of them were British, and most of them were American.

C I N E A S T E : *Like your films, the Ealing films are character-driven and have a certain modesty.*

L E I G H : Yes, there's a social context and they are comic. There's a broader British comic tradition. I grew up in the age of radio comedy, and then television comedy, as well as the movies. Certain of the Ealing films — *Kind Hearts and Coronets, The Man in the White Suit, The Lavender Hill Mob, Passport to Pimlico,* and Alexander Mackendrick's *The Lady Killers* — had a great impact on me. *Kind Hearts and Coronets,* for example, is one of the most perfectly told film stories and is brilliantly understated in a very English way. I don't know if that is one of the films I would have been conscious of at an early age because it came out around 1948, when I would have been around five. Whereas other films, like *The Man in the White Suit* and *The Titfield Thunderbolt,* were films I would have seen.

Later, by the time I was in my teens, you have those relatively inferior, still quite good, but sometimes politically suspect films of the Boulting

Alison Steadman, Roger Sloman, and Anthony O'Donnell, *Nuts in May*, 1976

Tim Roth, *Meantime*, 1983

Ruth Sheen and Philip Davis, *High Hopes*, 1988

Ruth Sheen, Edna Doré, and Philip Davis, *High Hopes*, 1988

Jane Horrocks and David Thewlis, *Life Is Sweet*, 1990

Alison Steadman and Jim Broadbent, *Life Is Sweet*, 1990

David Thewlis, *Naked*, 1993

Deborah Maclaren and David Thewlis, *Naked*, 1993

Greg Cruttwell and Katrin Cartlidge, *Naked*, 1993

Timothy Spall and Brenda Blethyn, *Secrets & Lies*, 1996

Mark Benton, Lynda Steadman, and Katrin Cartlidge, *Career Girls*, 1997

Brothers that followed the Ealing Comedies. Alec Guinness is replaced here by Peter Sellers, who was a great inspiration over a period of time. I think the best of those is a film called *Carlton-Browne of the F.O.,* which I think had a different title in America [*Man in a Cocked Hat*—ed.]. It's about an island in the middle of nowhere which becomes the center of international tension. Then, of course, the so-called British New Wave was going on.

C I N E A S T E : *Free Cinema?*

L E I G H : I didn't discover Free Cinema until after it happened because that was in the Fifties, when I was still a teenager in the provinces. Their work, as you know, led to the New Wave of *Saturday Night and Sunday Morning.* Having grown up in an urban world, it was exciting to know that there was a cinema attempting to deal with that, although one sometimes had reservations about whether it was quite real or slightly artificial. Then, quite unbeknownst to me—because in the Sixties I was operating in rather obscure corners of nowhere, doing odd things in basements—what was actually going on at that time was the early Ken Loach stuff, and Tony Garnett and all the *Wednesday Plays.* Tony Garnett later produced *Hard Labor,* my first television play following *Bleak Moments.*

I saw *Hard Labor* on television about two months ago. It's very much my film. It has some very personal things in it and it's autobiographical. Nevertheless, there are things in it that are completely uncharacteristic of my work—improvised footage, walking about in the market—things you wouldn't find in a film of mine before or after. Because Tony had worked so much with Ken Loach, there were things he encouraged and I was happy to become part of this *Play for Today* style. Honored, too, because these guys are older than me. It was fine, but it doesn't really belong in my films, it's not what I would do. I was very taken with Loach's films—I remember *Kes,* particularly. There are many ways in which Ken and I have a lot in common, and many ways in which we are at absolutely polar ends of the spectrum.

C I N E A S T E : *Are there political differences as well as cinematic differences?*
L E I G H : Politically, I'm sure that he would regard me as, at best, a lily-livered liberal. And quite rightly so.

C I N E A S T E : *Are there other contemporary British directors you admire?*
L E I G H : I have a lot of respect for Stephen Frears who, in the *Play for Today* era, was much more successful. He is a very good, eclectic director, and I think what he does is brilliant.

CINEASTE: *So an interest in film predated any interest in theater?*

LEIGH: Yes. I did see theater, but, without a shadow of a doubt, film was my main interest. Theater was always something there that you could do. I was involved with plays at school. You couldn't make films at school. Indeed, when I got involved with theater, it was because you could actually do it. It was there. You could make theater happen for nothing. You can't make films happen for nothing. It took a while to get sorted out. As soon as I trained as an actor, the first thing I did was to get work in really quite dreadful films, just so I could be there and see what happens.

CINEASTE: *What films did you act in?*

LEIGH: I was in a film called *Two Left Feet,* not to be confused with its singular successor, and some others.

CINEASTE: *We read a piece which talked about your films in terms of specifically Jewish humor, and the influence of your adolescent participation in the* Habonim *movement on your collaborative approach. Do you have any further comments on this?*

LEIGH: I have slightly mixed feelings about this, because I think it could be distracting and distorting. Very much in passing, however, it's possible to see a certain kind of Jewish influence. But I think it would be wrong to label these films "Jewish," or for a whole new kind of interpretation to grow out of this. I think it would be nonsense, I really do. On the other hand, given that there's a consistent tragicomic thing going on, it's possible that's a perspective you could put on it. The tragic moments always have a comic irony. In that sense, I could concede that as an element. There is a thesis on Pinter which says the same thing—his background is also Jewish—but it would be eccentric to say that Pinter is like Isaac Bashevis Singer.

CINEASTE: *Or it would be dangerous to say that this is some sort of hidden agenda.*

LEIGH: Yes. That's what worries me the most. In terms of a conscious or deliberate issue, the only film which deals with it at all—and that very marginally—is *Hard Labor.* The character is working for a Jewish man. He comes by to collect the money for the booth. For anyone to suggest that there is this Jewish or Zionist fifth column would be just ludicrous. In the Fifties, before Zionism became a dirty word, the *Habonim* was a left wing movement I was involved in as a kid and as a teenager. I walked away from all of those things, including the Jewish background, when I was seventeen. That organization was part of a propaganda machine to get us all to go live on a kibbutz. In fact, we did a lot of things cooperatively, and worked in groups. The positive thing—because I was as much of an individualist then as I am now—was that we did a lot of things collaboratively. This experience has, in some ways, informed my working with actors on film. Not that what I do is ultimately cooperative, because I'm very much in control of it. So all these matters should be put in a very distant perspective.

CINEASTE: *We'd like to ask about your play,* It's a Great Big Shame! *In many respects, this sounded as ambitious as* Naked, *and seemed to mark a similarly new direction.*

LEIGH: We worked on it very intensively for four months. It then ran for seven weeks. It is a deeply frustrating experience because it was a very elaborate production. There are plays of mine, particularly *Abigail's Party,* which are endlessly performed, and, in that way, still live. Indeed, it's on video, so you can see the original production. The new play is such an elaborate piece of theater, an integrated piece of pyrotechnics, that I think it would be extremely unlikely—even if we publish it—that it would ever be done much. It's kind of dead and buried, really. In the early days, I did lots of plays which are dead and buried. That's the nature of theater, as distinct from cinema. I suppose that because I've done mostly films, I've gotten used to the enduring nature of the thing.

CINEASTE: *Where did the idea of the juxtaposition of the Victorian story and the contemporary black characters' saga come from in* It's a Great Big Shame!?
LEIGH: Oddly enough, it came from a quite schematic notion. The Theatre Royal, Stratford East, in the East End of London, where it was produced, is a Victorian theatre. It's right in the middle of what is now a very multiracial, working class area. And it's remarkable that the theatre still stands. At one time, there were a number of such theatres all around the London metropolitan area. They've all disappeared, except that one. It's managed to keep going. They have a tradition of doing Victorian, music hall oriented shows.

CINEASTE: *And the modern story is your first extended treatment of black characters?*

LEIGH: It's the most extended treatment. You saw minor but important black characters in *Meantime,* and black characters have popped up now and then. To be perfectly honest, casting black actors has become easier with the rise of a new generation of young black British actors. For a long time, it was quite difficult to do this kind of work with black British actors. A lot of the older generation of black British actors, who had mostly come from the West Indies, were not necessarily the best. They were actors because they were black, not because they were actors. Also, a lot of black actors tended to be, as it were, more like white actors who wanted to be respectable.

Because you've got a generation of people who have been born in the U.K., there are now a lot of black actors. They've come out of ordinary schools in urban areas where drama is one of the subjects. Twenty years ago, if you wanted to see all the black actors in their twenties, you could probably conduct the auditions in a day or two. It would now take ages, so the standard is much higher. These are also very talented people who don't have a complex about being black. There's a great confidence about it. I worked on *It's a Great Big Shame!* with actors who were really very relaxed and funny. They have a real sense of roots but without being self-conscious and neurotic about it.

CINEASTE: *This resurgence of black British actors is not yet really noticeable in films.*
LEIGH: I don't think the films have happened yet, but they will. Isaac Julien has had a go. I hope others will be coming along.

CINEASTE: *You have become an influential director. Do you think that anyone has successfully emulated your approach to filmmaking?*
LEIGH: This is a delicate area. I'll go so far as to say this—if what I do works, it's because I'm a writer, or a filmmaker in that sense, not because of my technical skills. Technical skills are important, but primarily it's conceptual creation. The misconception on the part of some people is that if you follow a formula, you can come up with the same results. I don't think that's true.

An Interview with Mike Leigh

PRAIRIE MILLER/1996

THE INTERNATIONAL ACCLAIM FOR Mike Leigh's
Academy Award nominated *Secrets And Lies* has not yet quite died
down, but the British director is already stirring some new excitement with his latest movie *Career Girls*. The movie, which stars
Katrin Cartlidge, is about a reunion between old college friends,
and the funhouse mirror that is called memory. In person, Leigh
is as animated and impassioned as any his characters, and he
talked about these creations of his imagination with us as if they
are his closest and most treasured friends.

PRAIRIE MILLER: *Where did the idea for your film* Career Girls *come
from?*
MIKE LEIGH: You know, all my films are full of ongoing, running ideas.
It's not the kind of movie where there's one idea. And I'm fascinated, and
always have been, by the way you run into people after a long time and
they've changed, but they're still the same old them. It's about friendship,
and it's about caring for people. It's about memory and the way things
become fragmented that happened in the past. They're kind of things I've
dealt with before in my films in different ways, and I just thought it would
be good to look at this very specifically. I actually go back and see what
they were like, and share those things with the audience a bit.

This interview appeared in several on-line publications. © 1996 Prairie Miller. Reprinted
by permission of the author.

P M :   *Is* Career Girls *autobiographical?*

M L :   All my films are autobiographical, but not in a kind of specific way. I mean, I can't point to a particular character or event and say, that's me and that's what happened to me. But the spirit of my films are very much personal, and in that sense autobiographical.

I just am endlessly fascinated by the way that we change, we stay the same, we have these accumulated memories, and our memories become confused. And that there are certain passions for people that don't ever die. There's a bit of that explored in *Career Girls* and it's an important thing. Life is an untidy, unresolved, complicated bundle of order with a huge amount of disorder and bad timing. That's what I try to deal with in a small way in this film. We all have these experiences and feelings and they won't go away, and that's what it's about.

P M :   *Is there any particular character in* Career Girls *that you identify most with, or feel closest to?*

M L :   No. The funny and strange thing is, if I think of all my characters, I suddenly find that there's bits of me in all of them, really. It's one of those curious things. I mean, obviously, if you take Hannah, whom Katrin Cartlidge plays, there are aspects of the kind of humor and role playing, particularly when I was much younger, that I would identify with. But again, she's a different sort of person, she's a woman. Again, sometimes I feel like a very big lump that Ricky is, and sometimes I'm the sort of heel that the real estate agent is. It depends, really.

P M :   *With* Career Girls *and* Secrets And Lies, *you seem fascinated with female bonding, and maybe more interested than you are in male relationships. Could you say something about that?*

M L :   Not very much that's interesting. The truth is that as a storyteller and artist, I am concerned with Us, with the relations between men and women and the way we are, and all these things are important to me. There's no way that I can specifically tell you that I have a particular reason for being concerned with female relations as such. It's just something that's as important to me as everything else, really.

I mean I'm a gregarious, sophisticated, experienced person who's known a lot of people and actually known various kinds of women ranging from my grandmother and my mother through to my sister, and all kinds of other women that I've known in various other capacities, some biblical and some not. But mainly I'm a person whose job as an artist is to explore, discuss and tell stories about the human condition.

P M : *You call your movie* Career Girls, *and yet what we really see are the characters away from work, and never at their jobs.*
M L : Well, there's a certain irony in that. We see them a lot of the time in the film when they're students, and they're very much not career girls. And here they are in these official roles of career women, they've got it together. But actually it's not working in the strict sense for either of them, it's fractured in some ways. So they're playing this role, this career girl role, but again underneath it all, it's still the same old them a few years up the line. So that's why I've called it *Career Girls.* You don't see them in their work situation, because obviously I'm concerned with exploring their relationship with each other.

P M : *You're known for your unique method of organically crafting your scripts in collaboration with the cast. Do you ever feel this method distances you from your own original and personal conception of the story?*
M L : On the contrary, I cannot imagine working in a way that would allow me more ability to do what I want to do, and to explore more precisely what it is I want to explore. I think if I were to be forced by some fascist regime with a gun to my head to write scripts in a conventional way, I would then feel there was no way I could access what I really wanted to do. And to me the way I work, which I hope is getting more and more refined as time goes by, is very much a way of really being able to address what I really want to address, and make the film live and work just the way I want it to be. And it's because it's about filmmaking. It's not about writing a piece of literature, which you then convert into something called a film. It's about working, as it were, directly onto the canvas, creating the film in, as you say, an organic way, working from scratch. And that gives you absolute control over it. We're talking about filmmaking here, and any filmmaker that feels they are making a film by themselves frankly neither understands the medium nor is a genuine filmmaker. There's no such thing as a film that you make by yourself. It is a collaborative process, and all I do is shift the boundary lines a bit. Even if you write a script conventionally, other people are going to make that film with you, actors are

going to interpret those roles. So all I do is integrate the writing and conception of the film, the exploration, the research and all those things that lead to the film, with the actual organic process of making the film itself.

P M : *Has the popularity of your work affected you?*
M L : It just encourages me. I've been making films since 1971, and some of the films I've made have sunk into relative obscurity. That's not what I make films for.

P M : *Are you working on any other films right now?*
M L : No, goodness, I've just made this film since *Secrets And Lies*. I think that was pretty good going, really. You want another one as well? [We laugh.] It takes time, you know.

P M : *In* Career Girls *we see a lot of signs of physical distress, like rashes and tics, that literally 'flesh out' your characters. What about that?*
M L : Yes, I think it's no big deal. I mean, with all due respect to everybody, we're all susceptible to tics and twitches of one kind or the other. That's idiosyncratic, and that's how people are. The only reason why you may be prone to interpret or decode them as a series of statements, images or symbols of some kind is that on the whole characters in movies don't behave like real people.

On the whole, characters in movies behave like actors behave when they're playing characters in movies. Which is to say, with all the twitches, tics and behavioral and physical characteristics and defects removed and sort of blanded and bleached out of existence. Here I am simply putting people on the screen the way we really are, and so it may seem that it's all about tics and twitches, but it's just about people really.

P M : *Why did you want to become a filmmaker?*
M L : Why? Well, when I was twelve, on a very, very snowy and cold day in the middle of winter in Manchester, I stood in the front hall of my grandparents' house. My grandfather was carried downstairs in a coffin by four old men with drips at the ends of their noses. And my response to this tragi-comic occasion was the thought that it would be great to make a film about this. So that's not answering your question as to Why, but I'm just reporting on an impulse that came out of a particular moment and a

specific memory that may in some way answer that question. You know, you're an artist if you can draw or make music or whatever it is you can do, because you find that you can do it. And then you do it by compulsion, by need. I mean, I've never been the sort of filmmaker who's felt I had to kind of comply with this or that, to have a 'career' in something called movies. I'm not into that at all, I'm into doing something which is creative, organic, personal and idiosyncratic, which might have been drawing or painting or writing novels, and in fact is moviemaking. And I bless the fact to have been born in a time when the movies were around. I can't answer your question, except that it's a matter of compulsion, need, and urgency. You know, it's a disease.

P M :   *Well then maybe the question is, why are you suffering from this fascinating disease?*
M L :   I talk about grandpa's funeral as an answer to the question because although it's about the joy of watching movies, it's about doing something with life, and not just about making movies. That's my point. It's about the joy of putting real life and the texture of real life on the screen. It's people on the screen. Warts and all. Drips on the ends of old men's noses.

The Case for Mike Leigh

KENNETH TURAN/1996

SQUEEZED INTO A SURPRISINGLY small number of blocks, London's Soho district resembles a miniature city, a tiny metropolis with appetites both intense and specific.

Food is one, as a lifetime's worth of restaurants line the short streets. Sex is another, with strip clubs and licensed shops promising an "astonishing collection of adult publications including Amazons in Action" serving as a reminder of the area's red-light district past. And film is a third.

Twentieth Century-Fox and the William Morris Agency decorously share a squat brick building on one Soho corner ("Prepare for Impact!" says a noticeably British window poster for *Independence Day*), and numerous film company offices and post-production facilities such as De Lane Lea Sound Center are dotted throughout the area.

Slumping comfortably (a usual position) in a chair at an upstairs dubbing stage at De Lane Lea is a director putting the final touches on the soundtrack to a forthcoming film, still unfussily named *Untitled '96*. "We're now into the realms of higher Zen refinement now," he says with typical easy wit as he shares a laugh with his editor about an item in a London paper: Emily Bronte's *Wuthering Heights,* a reviewer said when the book came out in 1847, "will never appeal to general readers."

The director is 53-year-old Mike Leigh, considered by many critics the preeminent filmmaker in the English-speaking world. He's a man who works

From *The Los Angeles Times,* 22 September, 1996. © 1996 The Los Angeles Times. Reprinted by permission.

in a way completely and totally his own, going well below the surface to create an unmatched level of emotional intensity, and, in the process, stretching the boundaries of psychological truth on film as far as they will go.

Leigh's ability to work with actors and create characters of unequaled complexity is marveled at not only by critics but by the performers as well, even veterans of stage, television and film like Brenda Blethyn. "If I see myself on screen in a conventional scripted piece like *A River Runs Through It* (she played Brad Pitt's mother), I'm more analytical, wondering 'why am I looking like that, why did I make that choice?' But when I'm watching myself in one of Mike's films, I don't ever do that. I feel like I'm looking at a completely different person."

Even more remarkable than Leigh's impressive results is the unconventional and unlikely way these projects came into being. His way of working is so at variance with how Hollywood operates that despite the considerable interest he arouses in the industry, it's impossible to imagine Mike Leigh on a sound studio stage.

"I absolutely love his movies—it's mesmerizing filmmaking," says Laura Ziskin, who produced *To Die For* and numerous other Hollywood films before becoming president of Fox 2000, Twentieth Century Fox's newest film unit. "Though they aren't the kind of movies I can feed my machine, there's a kind of life there that keeps all of us on our toes and, hopefully, affects our work."

While conventional movies begin with the written word, Leigh doesn't put anything on paper until the film is shot and edited, and only then if a script is needed for book publication. Hollywood considers nothing more critical than matching actors to specific characters, but Leigh hires performers without knowing what their characters will be like. As for titles, *Untitled '96* indicates they come last of all.

"The thing about my job," says Simon Channing-Williams, Leigh's producer and partner in Thin Man Films Ltd., "is that I have to go to financiers and say, 'I'd like you to give us a very large amount of money, but I can tell you nothing about the project, not even who's in it.' It's a terrible leap of faith for them, and however much you explain how Mike works, they always say at some point, 'But there must be a script; you have to have a script.' They think what we've been saying is a game we perpetuate to create some sort of mystique." The producer allows himself a weary shake of the head at the foolishness of it all.

Leigh has made 14 feature-length films with his unique working methods over the past 25 years, and they've not gone unrecognized. *Life Is Sweet*, for instance, was named best picture of 1991 by this country's National Society of Film Critics, and 1993's *Naked* won the best director prize for Leigh and the best actor prize for David Thewlis at Cannes. Leigh's last three features have earned back their production costs (between $1 and $2 million) in the United States alone, doing better at the box office than the similarly budgeted British films of director Ken Loach.

The director was awarded an O.B.E. (Order of the British Empire) by Queen Elizabeth II in 1993 ("Terribly difficult at the moment, isn't it?" she commented about his profession) and producer Channing-Williams echoes what most objective observers agree on: "If he's not a genius, he's something bloody close to it." Yet despite all this, Leigh is still largely unknown by the average moviegoer in this country, a situation that is about to change in a big way.

Secrets & Lies, Leigh's latest film, has had the markings of a breakthrough since it won both the Palme d'Or and the International Critics Prize at this year's Cannes festival (plus the best actress prize for Brenda Blethyn) and followed that with a similar double at Australia's Sydney Film Festival, being named best picture by both the audience and critics. That kicked off the director's most commercially successful run across the U.K., where *Secrets & Lies* has already made more at the box office than his last three films combined, a feat paralleled by its being the first of Leigh's works to make a sizable impression worldwide, with rights sold in something like 100 countries.

In this country, *Secrets & Lies* debuted over the Labor Day weekend at the Telluride Film Festival and—accompanied by a biography, Michael Coveney's *The World According to Mike Leigh,* just published by Harper-Collins—is headed for Friday's prestigious opening-night slot at the New York Film Festival. The film opens in Los Angeles Oct. 4, and then, according to Bingham Ray, co-managing executive of American distributor October Films, it'll head gradually into about 150 markets. "We're going to play this to an extent no Mike Leigh movie has played before," says Ray. If, after decades of hellacious work, there is to be a moment for Mike Leigh to become an overnight success, it is now.

Paradoxically, Leigh's growing preeminence has surprised no one more than his fellow countrymen. Uniformly esteemed in America, the director has been subject to considerable criticism in Britain. The carpers run the gamut from those who question his work methods, claiming that he's exploiting the actors who obligingly "write" his films for him, to those who complain of what they perceive as a condescending attitude toward his characters.

Most vitriolic of these vilifiers was the late Dennis Potter, who insisted that Leigh's 1977 *Abigail's Party* was "based on nothing more edifying than rancid disdain, for it was a prolonged jeer, twitching with genuine hatred, about the dreadful suburban tastes of the dreadful lower-middle classes." And though his Palme d'Or victory has started to turn Leigh into "our Mike," before that, it was the rare British article about him that did not contain digs.

More than that, Leigh's success, like that of *Wuthering Heights,* has come in the face of considerable initial disbelief that such a thing was possible. He was told, for instance, that his working methods meant that "you can never get professional actors to do it." Yet he gave Tim Roth and Gary Oldman, both in 1983's *Meantime,* and Ben Kingsley, in 1973's *Hard Labour,* some of their first work.

Similarly, when Leigh talked to the BBC, for whom he made *Hard Labour* and seven other features, about shooting them on theatrical 35mm instead of made-for-TV videotape, "they didn't see it; it sounded like adolescent fantasizing to them." And though his most passionate following may be in the United States, Leigh remembers being told by American companies during his television years, "Your films of all films will not travel, and they especially will not travel to the United States."

Sitting in his comfortable Soho office located a floor below the intimate working environment of "Yvonne-French" and "Josett, formerly of Brewer Street," Leigh in person is a passionate, articulate man—friendly, yet wary, with a reflexive edge of asperity about him.

"You have to have your wits about you to work with him," says producer Channing-Williams. And Alison Steadman, who's appeared in several of his features, says, "Mike doesn't suffer fools gladly. If someone gets up his nose with a stupid remark, he will say so. He's quirky, not your run-of-the-mill Mr. Nice Guy, and he doesn't disguise his difficult side."

Yet Brenda Blethyn—who remembers him fooling with the sides of the box that his Cannes award came in, quipping, "These must be the doors of the Palme d'Or"—says he's "one of the funniest men on the face of the earth."

Overpowering all of these traits, however, is Leigh's compassion. "As a man, as a person, he's working from a loving, caring point of view," says Steadman, married to the director for more than 20 years. (The marriage is ending but the the two, who lived in a comfortable house in North London, remain on good terms.)

Journalists have commented on his resemblance to Charles Laughton, but with his full beard and deep, expressive eyes, Leigh looks surprisingly like a wonder-working Hasidic rabbi, able to examine the most intimate secrets of the soul.

Not surprisingly, Leigh makes films, as he said in accepting the Palme for *Secrets & Lies,* "about people, love, relationships, caring, real life—all the things that are important," what Leigh has called elsewhere "a lamentation and celebration of the human experience." Focusing on the awkward comic agony of life's unexpected crises, Leigh manages to exquisitely balance humor and pain without ever tipping over.

"My films," he says with energy, "aspire to the condition of documentary. If you're a newsreel cameraman and you go and shoot a real event, you know that that world exists whether you film it or not. What I want to do is create a world with that kind of solidity to it, something so three-dimensional and solid you could cut it with a knife." *Secrets & Lies* typifies the expert way Leigh zeros in on the emotional stress points of relationships. An examination of what happens when a young black woman named Hortense seeks out Cynthia, her white birth mother, it is laced with scenes that tear at the heart, none more so than their initial face-to-face meeting in a deserted London tea shop.

Cynthia (Brenda Blethyn), who gave her daughter up without even looking at her, initially thinks that Hortense (Marianne Jean-Baptiste) must be mistaken in thinking they are related. If she'd ever had sex with a black man, she says, she'd surely remember. Then, with awful suddenness, in a scene of exceptional emotional power, we see the memory literally flood Cynthia's face as she breaks down into convulsive sobs. "That moment is devastating," agrees *Secrets & Lies* cinematographer Dick Pope. "You can't believe it's acting, the emotion is so true."

The source of such a complex, heartfelt and unerringly realistic sequence is Leigh's celebrated, often misunderstood working method, the way he, in collaboration with his actors, uses a labor-intensive, improvisation-based system to, in effect, "grow" a film's characters from the ground up.

The director is fond of calling his method "organic," as in "growing properly rooted and centered," and his actors, making short work of the notion that they are exploited, are at a loss to find superlatives strong enough to describe the Great Adventure his films are for them. "An ultimate acting experience," says Brenda Blethyn. Katrin Cartlidge, who co-starred with David Thewlis in *Naked*, says: "It's not an acting job; it's a life experience, a profoundly fascinating and philosophical journey that's like climbing Mt. Everest."

The best way to understand how Leigh's method works and where it comes from is to examine the origins of the man. He grew up in Salford, a city next door to Manchester in the north of England, the grandson of Jewish immigrants. His father, who changed the family name from Liebermann to Leigh, was a doctor who was very much a part of the working-class area he lived and practiced in, and Leigh has vivid memories of the characters he either met or knew of, like the man who showed off a newspaper clipping headlined "Unknown Hoodlum Raids Bank" and boasted, "That's me!"

Even as a child, Leigh was a tremendous movie buff and always saw things in cinematic terms. "I used to make up films in my head, that was always my thing," he says. "I remember when I was 12 and my grandfather died, these ancient pallbearers were schlepping his coffin down the stairs. One of them had a long drip hanging from his nose, and I was thinking, 'You could make a movie out of this,' I remember just wanting to capture the spirit of it. My subject matter always is and was just looking at people the way they are."

Two other forces influenced the spirit of Leigh's work and his personality. One was simply growing up in the industrial North, a traditionally radical area with a strong working-class consciousness, where "people talk plain and direct. They don't mess about; they're in your face and honest."

The other factor, though Leigh has not often spoken of it, is his Jewishness in general and his having spent "my formative years in Habonim, a left-wing Jewish-Zionist youth organization" in particular. Since Habonim was "a kibbutz-oriented movement, I learned at an early stage about collaboration and sharing that, in a way, is how I work. I feel sometimes that I carry on a great Jewish tradition of a *rebbe* surrounded by Talmudic students, talking things out."

He insists on the caveat "at the most fundamental and obvious level it would be perfectly wrong to read my films as being primarily in any way about Jewishness" and says "for years and years I shut up about the whole thing, because you don't want to be labeled and the whole thing has a different currency in the English dimension."

But Leigh also knows that "on another, more sophisticated level it would be quite dishonest if I were to deny my films are Jewish in their way. The tragicomic view of life, the melancholy, if you know what you're talking about, there is a Jewish flavor to it, a Jewishness in the spirit of it. I could deny it, but it would be stupid."

Deciding that training as an actor would be the surest route to involvement in film, Leigh unnerved his parents by applying for and getting accepted at RADA, London's prestigious Royal Academy of Dramatic Art, in 1959.

During his brief time as an actor, Leigh managed bit parts in a few British films. Knowing he "just wanted to see film happening, no matter what the film was," Leigh hung out on movie sets, spent considerable time at the National Film Theatre and took classes at night at the London School of Film Technique.

Since it was easier to get directing jobs in plays than in films, much of Leigh's early experience was in the theater. He began his improvisatory methods with teenage actors at the Midlands Arts Centre in Birmingham in 1965, and he mentions a 1968 London play, *Individual Fruit Pies,* as the point at which he felt "I'd got how to do it: work separately with actors to create characters, gradually introduce them together, let it build and grow and then distill and refine."

Leigh's first film, 1971's *Bleak Moments,* was a theatrical feature taken from one of his stage plays and partly financed by Memorial Enterprises, the production company of fellow Salford native Albert Finney, who facetiously suggested *Carry on Gloom* for a title. Leigh is still pleased by the rave this story of a woman who struggles with the care of a mentally impaired sister got from a young Roger Ebert, who called it "a masterpiece, plain and simple," adding that "its genius is not just in the direction or subject, but in the complete singularity of the performances."

Given reviews like that, a career in theatrical features would seem a matter of course, but, in fact, Mike Leigh did not direct another film in 35mm until 1988's *High Hopes.* Though he now understands that *Bleak Moments* was "the fluke, the anomaly," he can't rid himself of the memories of all that time "when we made these films and nobody out there in the world knew about them. They'd be shown once and that was it. I went mad for 17 years. It was terrible."

Leigh directed nine made-for-television features during those years, almost all of them for the BBC. (Eight of these, including such Leigh classics as *Home Sweet Home* and *Grown-Ups,* are still available on video through Water Bearer Films, 800-551-8304). And these TV years did have their strong points. One was the enormous audience his films reached: The very popular *Abigail's Party,* for instance, was seen by about 9 million viewers in its *Play for Today* slot. More important was the opportunity for Leigh to fully learn the craft and perfect his method. "We complained about this and that, but the BBC was brilliant; it was good news," he says. "When I got the films, boy, it was carte blanche. Nobody ever interfered with casting or editing. I never made a cut that wasn't mine."

What started to change things for Leigh was the appearance as a potential financier of a new television entity, Channel 4, which rapidly became Britain's leading filmmaking institution. Channel 4 smartly shot its films in 35mm and made the decision to show them theatrically before their television debuts.

This was exactly the situation that Leigh had been looking for for years. Unfortunately, his first film for Channel 4 was shot before the decision was made to go to 35mm. That meant that 1983's marvelous *Meantime* was consigned to the video graveyard.

It was partly as a response to Leigh's growing success that the controversy about his treatment of the lower classes — a point of view that British film critics called patronizing, condescending and worse — began to build. But Leigh's collaborators, like cinematographer Dick Pope, are equally steadfast in his defense. "The British don't like to see themselves portrayed warts and all," he says flatly. "They find Mike a tricky customer. He gets under people's skins over here; he shows what's inside the dustbin."

Leigh, for his part, agrees that the criticism, which has no counterpart in other countries, says "more about England than about my films. This is a deeply class-ridden society like nowhere else, and everything resonates around that. Since I make films which are about England, because I'm specifically concerned with creating a real world, implicitly and inevitably, problems of class are part of the texture. People see what I do as a patronizing attack on the lower orders; they say it's wrong and immoral to patronize. But I'm not doing it, and Dickens didn't do it either."

The notion that there must be *something* written down is also something that refuses to die. *Secrets & Lies* actress Marianne Jean-Baptiste reports that "people keep talking about the script, asking what attracted me to the role of Hortense. There was no role—what you're attracted to is the process."

Similarly persistent and wrongheaded are the notions that Leigh's actors improvise on camera, or that the whole process is loose, mellow and unstructured. "It's no happening," retorts Leigh acerbically. "It's a great deal of order and discipline."

This lack of understanding is part of the reason, along with a sense of boredom, that Leigh talks about how he works with some reluctance. Also pushing him to hold his tongue is his belief that "in the end, the only thing that matters is what is on the screen; everything else is neither here nor there."

If there is a key to understanding Mike Leigh's process, it lies, in a typical paradox, in forgetting how smart and articulate the man is. In every aspect of his work, Leigh is intuitively depending almost exclusively on instincts too basic and fluid to stand articulation. On a profound level, asking him how he does what he does makes no more sense than asking a novelist how he writes or a painter where his canvases come from.

What comes first, as it would with a more conventional writer, is the vaguest of notions, something that hovers in the air. Sometimes, as with *Secrets & Lies,* where Leigh knew he wanted to deal with adoption, the notion is fairly concrete. At other times, it's not.

"I'm always walking around with certain feelings and ideas kicking around, and I put myself in the position any artist can understand: Here is the space, here is the canvas. Every decision I make, starting with choosing actors, gives you different combinations, stimulates you. What I'm doing is looking for the film, testing what is going on against what I think I'm doing. It's an elusive combination of what I know and what I don't know, and no one should underestimate the importance of the fact that I'm only answerable to myself, even if I don't know what I'm doing."

Cast selection has a paramount position in Leigh's method. As Steadman says, "the act of choosing the first actor is for him like an artist choosing the first brush stroke."

"They've got to be intelligent, have a sense of humor and be good character actors, able to play something other than themselves," Leigh says. "And they've got to have a sense of the real world, to be fascinated by everybody and everything."

"Not every actor can do it," says actress Katrin Cartlidge, who appeared in *Naked*. "You can't be primarily interested in what your role is or how famous you're going to be. You need a huge amount of patience and the ability, if possible, to keep paranoia well and truly out the door and under lock and key." Adds Steadman: "You need a terrific commitment to the work. It's no use thinking you're going to have much social life or much family life. The work just does take up so much time."

The process, which Cartlidge describes as being "like going on a journey blindfolded, feeling your way along," always begins with Leigh working one-on-one with each of the actors in a joint quest to find the character that can last up to two or three months. These sessions are strictly private, as is all of Leigh's process. They begin with talk of people the actor knows, even casually, and proceed, via questions and discussion, to expand on characteristics and possibilities. It all leads to the moment when the director chooses someone to focus on.

Now comes the laborious work of fleshing that choice out that sets Leigh's work apart. Every imaginable facet of the character from infancy onward—from "when you learned to swim to what color toothbrush you use," according to David Thewlis—is brought up and discussed in detail with the director. "You build up memories, experiences, a whole life that becomes almost as real to you as the one you live yourself; it infiltrates the fabric of your subconscious," says Cartlidge, who reports, as does Thewlis, that she actually began dreaming as her character as the process intensified.

The work actors do in this regard is physical as well as mental. Since Brenda Blethyn's Cynthia in *Secrets & Lies* worked 10-hour shifts in a box factory, the actress did so as well and also spent time in libraries reading newspapers about her character's formative years. And since daughter Hortense was an optometrist, actress Marianne Jean-Baptiste went to a university to study optometry three times a week for three months.

This verisimilitude continues during actual filming. On 1976's *Nuts in May*, about the adventures of an eccentric couple on a camping vacation, Leigh insisted that Steadman and Roger Sloman, who played the pair, follow their vacation plan even when he was not filming them. "So we had to put on our costumes, go into character, and take a 15-mile up-and-down hike around Lulworth Cove in Dorset. It was tiring and exhausting, we were in character all day, and I honestly didn't think I was going to make it."

All this differs, the actors emphasize, from the more common acting practice of working out a backstory, a "past," for a character. "I could create an entire history for Lady Macbeth and nobody would ever be the wiser," says Cartlidge. "Your responsibility is far greater here. I'm being invited by Mike to use every ounce of my creative and imaginative soul to provide the fabric that goes into the making of this film."

And it's not only the leads. Every character in a Mike Leigh film is this carefully worked out. On the earlier *Life Is Sweet*, *Naked* star David Thewlis admits to having felt "disgruntled and paranoid" when it turned out that he had only a small part as the boyfriend of Nicola, a character played by Jane Horrocks. "All I did was come in, cover Jane Horrocks with chocolate and lick it off. I'd done all this work, and they could have gotten anyone off the street to do that—no offense to Jane."

(Because Leigh insists that characters, even if related, know only as much about each other as they would in real life, Steadman, who played Horrocks' mother, was shocked to find out at *Life Is Sweet*'s first screening what her daughter had been up to with all that chocolate. "I said, '*What? She was doing what?*' Whenever I'd come home, her character would be in the bath, but I suspected the problem was that she had a washing disorder. It turns out I'd gotten the wrong end of the stick, as we do in life.")

Once Leigh decides that his characters are at the appropriate stage of readiness, the director brings them together for more months of extensive improvisations. "Actors can be very afraid of it, because you're very vulnerable; you can make a fool of yourself," says Steadman. "But when Mike sets one up, he makes sure the actor has all the relevant information, so you feel 100% secure in your imagination." To emphasize this, Steadman says, Leigh at a certain point will set up what he calls The Quiz Club for his actors. "We all gather in a room and he asks us questions which we answer only in our heads. 'What does your character think about Margaret Thatcher?' 'What does he or she think about sex before marriage?' 'What did you give for Christmas presents?' When you realize you are secure enough in your character to answer all these questions, you know that everything's clear and watertight."

Leigh, in fact, expects you to know the person you play so inside out that, during the filming of *Secrets & Lies,* he bawled out Blethyn when another character drank out of the wrong mug in a scene set in her kitchen, ruining two hours of filming. "It wasn't a continuity problem; it was my problem. He gave me a striping in front of everyone," says Blethyn, still a bit shaken at the memory. "He said I lived in the house—I should know which cups I had. He expects that precision from everyone."

Even though your character may be ready for improvisation, the character Leigh intends you to interact with may not. Or the director may be busy with some of the film's other characters. But it's always possible that you'll suddenly be wanted on short notice. It is this need to be on standby for what can be weeks on end, "waiting around like a doctor on call while keeping your character on the boil," says Cartlidge, that leads to the unavoidable bouts of paranoia that all Leigh's actors experience.

"You start thinking, 'He's not impressed with my work, he doesn't think I'm right, I'm not serving any purpose,'" remembers Thewlis. Even Blethyn, who turned out to be the star of *Secrets & Lies,* says there were moments when "I started to think, 'I'm not going to be in this film.' If Mike would be working elsewhere I'd say to myself, 'I bet the whole cast is in that bit, I'll bet that's what the film is about.'" As Cartlidge says, "you need to have nerves of steel."

Though they start with the characters meeting each other cold, these improvisations, which regularly go on for hours, can have explosive results. Perhaps because of the incendiary nature of its story, the strongest improv tales come out of *Naked,* the harrowing story of a nightmarish few days a sullen Manchester drifter named Johnny (played by Thewlis) spends in London.

One of Johnny's street encounters is with an equally hot-tempered Scottish vagrant named Archie (Ewen Bremner, who went on to play Spud in *Trainspotting*). "In the initial improvisation on a London street, we became very hostile," Thewlis remembers. "There was a lot of shouting, beer cans were thrown, one of us had a screwdriver and wanted to fight— it got a little dangerous. Then Mike came over and very quietly said, 'Come out of character' and we're required to shut up. All these people watching must have thought, 'What did this little character in the beard say to these hoodlums?' Then the police came along and Mike had to

explain his work methods and walk back to the rehearsal rooms to produce his documents from Channel 4."

Equally intense was Johnny's interaction with a woman named Sophie
(played by Cartlidge), his former girlfriend's roommate. "There was an
instant rapport between our characters, and though we'd never met before
as actors, we ended up kissing and exploring each other's bodies," Thewlis
reports. "Then Mike said, 'Come out of character,' and there was a moment
when she held out her hand and said, 'Hello, I'm Katrin.' We were terribly
shy with each other then—our first conversation was so stilted. She's since
become one of my dearest friends, but it was the strangest start to, hopefully, a lifelong friendship you could imagine."

With uncounted hundreds of hours of improvisations to choose from, it
is Leigh's particular genius to know exactly which sequences and moments
are worth saving, reconsidering and paring down. So much of the success
of his method depends on this ability that Leigh himself admits that
"though, in the early days, I would tend to proselytize about it, what I
actually specifically do is so idiosyncratic that I suspect it is exclusively
useful to me." Though he never writes out anything more than bare one-
line outlines of scenes, once he hears what he wants in a sequence, Leigh
expects his actors to recall their words for the camera exactly the way
they've rehearsed them. Unlike the work of John Cassavetes, for instance,
absolutely no spontaneous speech is allowed once filming begins, a situation that demands that actors be able to switch from the free-flow of
rehearsal to absolute precision.

While Leigh is happy to name American actors like Jennifer Jason Leigh,
who he's confident could work for him, the intensity of his methods
makes it unlikely that major Hollywood stars would fit in, and it's something of a parlor game among his actors to imagine what that interaction
would be like. Steadman, for instance, comically widens her eyes to indi-
cate sincerity and mimics, "They might say, 'Believe me, I'm ready, this is
what I want,' but a week in they'd be saying, 'What is this? I'm Brad Pitt,
I'm not doing a 15-mile hike on Lulworth Cove.'"

As for Leigh himself, those same methods, plus his insistence on brook-
ing absolutely no interference, means that no matter how much
Hollywood might be fascinated by what he does, asking if he could make
films here is pointless. "What I do is very narrow, very rarefied, very spe-

cific," he says. "It's not portable, so why would I want to shoot myself in the foot and work in Hollywood? I'd rather drink arsenic or ground glass and get it over with quickly." But if a way could be found to furnish Leigh with ironclad guarantees of autonomy, he would accept Hollywood's money, because the thoroughness of his labor-intensive methods does not come cheap. When the talk returns to that marvelous tearoom scene between mother and daughter in *Secrets & Lies,* Leigh suddenly raises his voice over the din of a Soho night seeping through closed windows to make his point.

"That film cost over £3 million, and people might say, 'Where's the value for money? Where's the helicopter shots?' That scene is where. You can only do that kind of stuff because of weeks and weeks of preparation, of building history. Anyone can get two actresses in a room and say, 'She's your mother, improvise,' but it'll still be crap. We've lived through it all, we built it all, and it all earns its keep. That time spent gestating is value for money, and nobody gets it for nothing."

Not even Mike Leigh—

An Original Who Plumbs the Ordinary

ALAN RIDING/1996

STRANGE CHAP, MIKE LEIGH. He quite bristles at the suggestion that his latest and most acclaimed movie to date is less bleak and
disturbing than most of his previous work. Well, sorry, Mike, *Secrets and
Lies,* which opens the New York Film Festival on Friday, *is* a positive film,
and it is funny and moving, too. But that, apparently, is not the point. The
53-year-old Englishman likes to quote Jean Renoir's dictum that every
director keeps reshooting the same film. So, he contends, while his mood
may change, his fundamental vision of life does not.

There, he is right. In a long career in theater, television and movies,
Mr. Leigh has peered constantly into a world almost of his own making. It
is a world readily seen in the homes, pubs and supermarkets of suburban
England, a world of humor, pain, love, loneliness and anger marked above
all by its ordinariness. But he has captured it with a true master's eye,
becoming in the process one of the most original filmmakers today. And
just as life may suddenly imitate a Bergman or a Fellini movie, Mr. Leigh's
world has now taken his name. After London tabloids recently broke the
story of a single mother pregnant with eight babies, one newspaper's head-
line read: "Mandy, her lover, her publicist and the doctor: it has the tragedy
and farce of a Mike Leigh film."

This, too, is the world of *Secrets and Lies.* Hortense (played by Marianne
Jean-Baptiste), a well-educated young black woman who was adopted by a

---

black family at birth, sets out to discover her real mother, who turns out to be white. The mother, Cynthia (Brenda Blethyn), a factory worker and single mother in her 40's, thinks at first that it is a mistake. But she never saw her first baby before adoption, and she finally remembers that one of her teen-age sex partners was black. Mother and daughter soon bond, while Cynthia keeps the secret of Hortense from her second daughter and the rest of her family, who in any event are busily engaged in the micromanagement of their own lives.

"It's a film about identity, about the need to connect, to share," Mr. Leigh explained recently. "We all have secrets and lies. If there's any message in this film, it is that you're better off telling the truth."

On the surface, with their laughter and tears, Mr. Leigh's stories resemble soap operas. Of course, the same can be said of Chekhov's plays or Jane Austen's novels or Rossini's operas. But the Devil is in the details, as they say. And in Mr. Leigh's case, what distinguishes the maestro from the hack is the extraordinary depth of his characters and the authenticity of the locations. By the time his films reach the screen, nothing is accidental, yet everything seems natural. It is something that great painters can achieve. It is something that Mr. Leigh has been striving for since he made his first movie, *Bleak Moments* in 1971.

Still, *Secrets and Lies* may eventually be remembered as his breakthrough film. Mr. Leigh's last movie, *Naked,* won awards for best director and best actor (David Thewlis) at the 1993 Cannes film festival. *Secrets and Lies* went a step further by winning the prestigious Palme d'Or and the best-actress award for Ms. Blethyn at this year's Cannes festival. But with *Secrets and Lies,* Mr. Leigh seems to have found a way of reaching a broader audience. More important, it has finally won him recognition as a world-class artist—both dramatist and director—in an England that until now has not known what to make of him.

Mr. Leigh's doleful eyes and unsmiling irony might suggest that he is tired of being misunderstood, but he is evidently proud that he does not fit in here. After all, he is viewed as an outsider, not because he is a Northerner whose flat Lancashire accent can still be detected or because he is Jewish or because he is by nature a bit of a loner, but rather because he has always stubbornly gone his own way. He has frequently clashed with such cultural icons as the BBC and the Royal Shakespeare Company. He has irritated movie industry colleagues with his idiosyncrasy, and he has earned the wrath of critics. But he has refused to bend to convention.

What perhaps first distinguished him as an artist was his unusual technique for building his stories, as much for theater as for cinema. Starting without a script or even much of a story line, he works one-on-one with his actors until they have invented the entire lives of the characters they are to play. He then has them improvise scenes with other characters who have been similarly created. Only after endless rehearsals does a final plot—and a script—take shape. It is a time-consuming technique, one that may tie up an actor for six months or more, yet actors who work with him invariably find it rewarding.

"I would regard it as a required experience for actors," said Stephen Rea, the Belfast-born star of Neil Jordan's *Crying Game* who has appeared in one play and two films by Mr. Leigh. "I know that not all actors take to it, but I somehow think that if you haven't done it, there's something lacking in your experience because you build a character literally from nothing." Ms. Jean-Baptiste, who was in Mr. Leigh's play *It's a Great Big Shame!* before playing Hortense in *Secrets and Lies,* agreed. "People don't work with Mike because of a role or a part," she said. "They work with him because of the process."

Once Mr. Leigh's plays and films have been presented to the public on the other hand, they have frequently provoked contradictory reactions here for reasons that are peculiarly English. Mr. Leigh's admirers abroad have no trouble recognizing the universal features of the family dramas that he portrays. And they are not required to identify the variety of non-BBC accents that may be employed. But to the English, particularly middle-class opinion makers, Mr. Leigh is dabbling with a subject as sensitive to them as, say, race is to Americans: the class system.

In a sense, this has been done before in the angry "kitchen sink" dramas and movies of the late '50s and early '60s. Yet in contrast to the work of, say, Karel Reisz or Lindsay Anderson, Mr. Leigh insists that he has no political agenda. He has made three films with some political content—*Meantime,* about unemployment; *Four Days in July,* about Northern Ireland's troubles, and *High Hopes,* about the loss of hope in the Thatcherite England of the 1980's—but in each case he said he was more interested in the lives of the characters he created. The charge against him, though, is not that he is some sort of leftist subversive. It is far more complicated. It is that, in portraying the lives of what many English still call the lower classes, he has been patronizing.

The late Dennis Potter fired the first shot at Mr. Leigh's 1977 play, *Abigail's Party,* which he described as "a prolonged jeer, twitching with genuine hatred, about the dreadful suburban tastes of the dreadful lower middle classes." Variations on this theme were frequently echoed by critics in upscale English newspapers who, uncomfortable at being shown behind the cheap curtains of humble homes, concluded that Mr. Leigh was making fun of the people living inside.

"This patronizing stuff is, so far as I'm concerned, so ludicrous and stupid and misinformed that there's not much I can say about it," the stocky, bearded director said in an interview in his office in Soho, one floor below an apartment occupied by a trio of well-mannered French prostitutes. "It doesn't worry me. It worries certain kinds of people and journalists. So-called working-class people do not have that problem with my work. I am naturally drawn to people with ordinary working lives. I think it important to make films about a side of life that films don't normally deal with."

His actors are also quick to jump to his defense. "The great thing about Mike is that he can still annoy people," said Timothy Spall, who plays Cynthia's photographer-brother, Maurice, in *Secrets and Lies.* "He's often accused of being patronizing to the working classes, but he is only accused by the middle classes, which is interesting." Mr. Rea, who appeared in *Four Days in July* said no one in Belfast felt patronized by the way Mr. Leigh portrayed Northern Irish families caught up in sectarian violence. "As for *Secrets and Lies,*" he said, "I think it is a kind of celebration of getting through misery with dignity."

Still, for the moment, all this is in the past. When *Secrets and Lies* was released in Britain last May, it was as if a new Mike Leigh had been discovered. "Gone is the self-conscious negativism, gone is the cold doctrinaire habit of caricature that used to put together a set of neurotic mannerisms and call the result a person," Adam Mars-Jones wrote in *The Independent.* "It isn't unprecedented for a Mike Leigh film to contain positive emotion. But *Secrets and Lies* has a positive philosophy of emotion, and that is new." Writing in *The Financial Times of London,* Nigel Andrews also sounded relieved. "Leigh has sneaked a human universality, an Esperanto of beatific bewilderment, into his plot," he said.

Mr. Leigh's response to these plaudits is typically downbeat. "I still have to get a night's sleep and go to the loo in the morning, and I still have the daunting prospect of making another film," he said, as if his chosen career were something of a sentence. "At earlier stages, when my films won prizes and it seemed like that was success, I was happy. Now, if this is a greater success, it rather reduces the earlier successes to a lesser success, but that's fine because at the time they seemed all right and now it's something else."

Mr. Leigh actually talks like that, in a convoluted way, as if improvising a response, feeling his way. He heads off in one direction, stops, turns around, decides he needs to condition his thought with "notwithstanding" or "however," sets off again "in a slightly roundabout way," and then perhaps concludes with, "nevertheless, finally, when the chips are down, as far as I'm concerned." It sounds as if it is quite complicated to be Mike Leigh. His syntax may even be an appropriate metaphor for his career. He has made it, but it has not been easy.

Born in Salford on the outskirts of Manchester in 1943, Mr. Leigh was raised in a Jewish household. His paternal grandfather, Mayer Lieberman, who migrated from Russia in 1902, was a portrait miniaturist who colored photographs. His father, who changed his German-sounding surname to Leigh in 1939, was a doctor. Young Mike's home was comfortable, but the grimy industrial town outside his front door was decidedly working class. So, from an early age, two ingredients of his subsequent work were already present: what he calls their Jewish "tragic-comic quality" and their working-class environment.

As a teenager, he loved movies and remembered acting in plays while a member of the socialist Jewish youth movement. In 1961, he won a scholarship to the Royal Academy of Dramatic Art, but he was not happy there. He was "a sullen and disruptive student," Michael Coveney writes in his new biography, *The World According to Mike Leigh*. In London, though, he expanded his horizons, discovering the writing of Samuel Beckett and Harold Pinter and the experimental work of Peter Brook, John Cassavetes and Joan Littlewood. He was particularly inspired by a television documentary about Mr. Brook's production of Peter Weiss's *Marat/Sade,* which showed actors going to an insane asylum and each basing his or her character on an inmate.

"At that point, I thought, if you can do all that to serve a play, then surely you can go one step further and make one up," he recalled. "And that's how I sort of decided that I wanted to work in a fairly instinctive and intuitive way. I don't think I have ever made an intellectual decision about anything, certainly not that."

After the Royal Academy, he created three plays with inner-city youths at the Midlands Art Center in Birmingham. In 1967, he was invited to be an assistant director at the Royal Shakespeare Company, working alongside Trevor Nunn in Peter Hall's production of *The Taming of the Shrew.* During his spare time, he created a play of his own by improvising with actors from the company. But if the experience at Stratford-on-Avon proved crucial, it was in convincing him that he did not want a traditional career as a theater director. He felt that his vocation was to tell stories and his dream was to do so in movies. Finally, in 1971, he made *Bleak Moments.*

But during most of the '70s and '80s, the British movie industry was moribund, and Mr. Leigh was limited to working in the theater and making films for the BBC. It was not until *High Hopes* in 1988 that he could raise the money necessary to return to the big screen, even with low-budget movies. By then, though, while little known abroad, his biting stories about English society had begun to cause waves here. His rehearsing and directing techniques had also stirred interest within the acting profession. Ms. Blethyn recalled that when she was invited to work on his television film, *Grown-Ups,* her agent told her: "This is the best job you've ever been offered." As with *Secrets and Lies* 16 years later, though, she had no inkling as to her role.

In fact, because Mr. Leigh wants his actors to know only what their characters would know in real life, he tells them little about the story. He creates situations that bring them together, but he wants them to be surprised. He even writes "Top Secret" on the daily shooting script. So in *Secrets and Lies,* while Ms. Blethyn spent long weeks creating her character, she only discovered that Cynthia's first daughter was black when she improvised her first meeting with Ms. Jean-Baptiste's Hortense ("You've got to laugh, ain't you, sweetheart, else you'd cry," says Cynthia, completely overwhelmed). And Ms. Blethyn only understood the entire story when she saw the edited film on the screen.

Mr. Leigh himself is quite happy if, even at the end, questions are left unanswered. "I do not make films which are prescriptive, and I do not make films that are conclusive," he said. "You do not walk out of my films with a clear feeling about what is right and wrong. They're ambivalent.

You walk away with work to do. My films are a sort of investigation. They ask questions; they're reflecting."

If his approach has not changed in 25 years, it is unlikely to change now. He recently completed a $1.9 million film, still untitled, about two women in their 30's looking back to their student days. And if he would like bigger budgets for future films (even *Secrets and Lies,* his most expensive film to date, cost only $4.5 million), it is simply to spend even longer on preparations and rehearsals. Certainly, for all the early success of *Secrets and Lies,* he has no illusions about working in Hollywood.

"I think it would be a disaster," he said. "Actually, it's absurd to think I could have total artistic freedom. Sometimes I hear that some studio is interested in me. Then they discover that this is the guy who works with no script, that there is no casting discussion, no interference, that I have the final cut, and that does it." He looked pleased with himself. Evidently, he has no plans to start fitting in now.

Rehearsals Hold Key to Mike Leigh Films

HOWIE MOVSHOVITZ/1996

ENGLISH DIRECTOR MIKE LEIGH, at the Telluride Film Festival last summer to receive a tribute and show his latest film, *Secrets and Lies,* had been asked so often about how he prepares movies that he gave the short answer:

"I cast a group of actors and gather them together and tell them in principle what we're going to do—and (really) tell them nothing. And then we proceed to do it. In this case, we took five months before we started shooting."

Leigh, maker of *High Hopes, Life Is Sweet,* and *Naked,* has been working like this for years. He begins with only the rudiments of a picture—the actors and sketchy ideas for their characters.

In rehearsals, they develop characters and situations. Complex relationships and events emerge from the work. Eventually, the cinematographer joins the group, and the growing film takes visual shape. By the time Leigh is ready to shoot, he has written the script, and everyone knows what's going on. But it has all happened since rehearsal began.

Secrets and Lies starts with Hortense at her mother's funeral. Soon afterward, Hortense, who'd been adopted at birth, searches for her birth mother. That turns out to be Cynthia, a weepy, middle-age woman sharing a crummy, narrow row house with Roxanne, another daughter. The two live in intimate misery and strife. Cynthia also has a brother, Maurice, a suc-

From *The Denver Post,* 3 November 1996. © 1996, 1997 The Denver Post. Reprinted by permission.

cessful photographer and a man of immense goodwill who looks after Cynthia and Roxanne.

And because no one has it easy in Leigh's world, Maurice and his wife, Monica, grieve secretly over their infertility.

Leigh is the son of a doctor who grew up in a working-class section of Manchester. He's moved to London and become a film director, but his material still comes from the people around whom he grew up, people whose circumstances range from barely modest to desperate, and who would like to do better.

Many of Leigh's characters combine the desire for money and better homes with callousness and rotten taste. His middle-class couple in *High Hopes* are positive horrors of acquisitive snobbery, and Maurice, at least, seems distant. So I asked Leigh if he distrusted wealth. He gave the kind of answer that shows how well he knows his characters and his material.

"It's complex," he said. "First of all, I think it's clear that Maurice is terribly busy. Basically, I think it's that. And part of what motivates the distance is the pure hostility between Cynthia and Monica (Maurice's wife), and obviously he is in the middle, and that would make him procrastinate.

"Again, I'm exploring what I've explored in various ways, the problem of upward mobility. (But they're not like) the couple in *High Hopes* who are undoubtedly grotesque and lampooned. Both Monica and Valerie (of *High Hopes*) are frustrated, but Valerie is neurotic to the extreme, extremely unfocused and extremely disoriented.

"Monica is none of those things—and she also has some kind of taste. (Valerie dresses like the queen.) Monica's other problem has basically to do with her condition. Not only is she infertile, but she has a monthly problem related to it."

Then Leigh summed up.

"I don't have a problem with wealth. The question is what they do with it and how they live and how honest they are and all those other things. If I didn't like wealth, I would give away what I get paid for directing motion pictures to various people. I do that to some extent, but I keep some of it because I have children (laughs). This is not a film about what wealth does to people. *High Hopes* is. This one has different concerns."

Almost everyone in *Secrets and Lies* has something hidden that has festered over the years. By the time Hortense shows up—her presence shakes the rest of the family to the bones — you can see how everyone has been dragged down by the emotional energy it takes to conceal and pretend.

It happens to most of us, and this accumulating of emotional baggage seems to be a common part of aging.

Leigh agreed.

"I have a lurking suspicion that most of my films are about that. *High Hopes* is certainly about that. *Life Is Sweet* undoubtedly deals with that. In *Naked* (Johnny, the ranter played by David Thewlis) refers to his age and to his death.

"It's a preoccupation of mine. The passing of time. If somebody writing a thesis went through my films looking for references to time, they'd find a helluva lot of it, explicitly and implicitly. This film is, of course, about that."

Mike Leigh films cut close to the bone. He shows shocking events and characters who aren't necessarily people his viewers would like to invite for dinner. He rejects heroes and villains because life doesn't break down that way and he finds it more interesting to see the complexity of human personality.

And, perhaps more dangerously, Leigh believes in a profoundly comic vision of human struggle. Life in all its problems is also funny. These attitudes leave Leigh's films open to remarkable misinterpretations because viewers often think that to depict a character is to approve of what the character does, and that laughter means Leigh isn't serious.

Leigh said he's been shocked that some people — with no evidence — believe that Roxanne is the daughter of an incestual relationship between Maurice and Cynthia. His films in general are often read as statements on how Thatcherism ravaged the British working class.

Naked, Leigh said, "was accompanied by degrading crap of a quasi-feminist kind, which called the film misogynist and me misogynist, which is plainly ridiculous. It takes a serious misreading of the film, to the point of naive stupidity."

And, often, viewers get lost in the struggles and don't see the obvious.

"*Secrets and Lies*," Leigh said, "is also about goodness."

The Leigh Way

RAY PRIDE/1996

IN MIKE LEIGH'S 1993 *Naked,* a brilliant thundercrack of a movie, a good filmmaker suddenly revealed himself as a great one. But like another important voice in international cinema, Robert Altman, Leigh's accomplishments are often clouded by false assumptions about his idiosyncratic work methods. Down-in-the-dumps playwrights and screenwriters like to repeat the ontological fairytale to one another that many audiences believe the actors make up their dialogue as they go along. In fact, Leigh and his actors do make it up as they go along, but they go along for a very long time. In the case of his largest-budgeted film to date, the $5-million *Secrets and Lies,* the cast spent eighteen weeks rehearsing starting in November 1994, followed by thirteen weeks of shooting, ending in July of last year.

The result of this arduous process—which Leigh admits leaves him bone-tired on the first day of actual shooting—is an exuberant, beautifully structured and acted story of an adopted young professional woman's search for her biological mother after the death of her adoptive mom. It's a Cinderella story, but with a twist.

Leigh's concern with class is subtler than usual, and, purposely, according to the filmmaker, the issues of race never come to bear on the conflict—there is already too much pain and too much thwarted love. It's an extraordinary piece of work, even if it never hits the apocalyptic highs of *Naked.*

Secrets and Lies is the forty-sixth stage or film production Leigh has assembled in his painstaking fashion. Leigh's technique, put in a reductive

From *New City* (Chicago), 7 November 1996. Reprinted by permission.

way he would surely resent, is to begin with a few themes and ideas, then branch out during lengthy rehearsals with his actors—singly and together, in real-life situations and in rehearsal halls, each knowing only as much as their character would know—into investigations of possible directions each character's life could take. (The process can go wrong. Leigh once abandoned a play, as well a television film in 1986, when the pieces did not crystallize after seven weeks.) The distillation process results in a discomfiting intimacy that may be what some critics resent. As the actors work with Leigh, they delve further into what they hide beneath their own daily carapace, managing to suggest worlds beyond the two hours we're watching.

In the just-released biography *The World According to Mike Leigh* (Harper-Collins, $24), author Michael Coveney describes watching an early hour of scenes from *Secrets and Lies* that gave little indication of the important characters and themes found in the finished work. The emphasis shifts as Leigh shoots and edits. From the set of *Secrets and Lies,* Coveney described Leigh's shooting script as a list of seventy or so scenes marked up on a double-sided, five-by-four-inch piece of foamboard that fit snugly in the filmmaker's shirt pocket.

On a 1970 award application, Leigh offered a rationale for his method-in-the-making: "I saw that we must start off with a collection of totally unrelated characters (each one the specific creation of its actor), and then go through a process in which I must cause them to meet each other, and build a network of real relationships; the play would be drawn from the results." He also took solace in the wisdom of Peter Brook, who said that each new task of directing is like starting out blind on an unknown journey.

His biographer writes, "[The work] was rehearsed and rehearsed until it achieved the required quality of 'finish.' There was, Leigh now knew, no such thing as an aimless direction. It was always a question of the end product, the final fiction, the story, the lives and the characters. And the supply of material was both unquantifiable and endless." (Still, Leigh once told a questioner at a post-play discussion, "I'm not interested in anything as much as the end product; I don't give a fuck about the processes.")

Leigh's work has always been composed of wicked-yet-poignant lampoon. He celebrates the peculiar, the idiosyncratic, the unique that sets a character apart from the fray. Some writers mistake his approach for caricature, but in virtually all of his films, a love for his wounded world shines through. It's difficult to see how critics can mistake Leigh's artful arraying of archetypes for anything but compassion. He seems in the tradition of Dickens as a writer, but as a filmmaker, he falls in line with Renoir, Ozu, Satyajit Ray, depicting ordinary lives with elegance and economy. His is a gourmand's appreciation, always showing a willingness to pause, to savor.

While the collaboration with his actors seems to take the collegial ideal of theatre to a radical extreme, Leigh's unassuming visual knack often goes unappreciated. Similarly, his classically structured works are filled with juxtapositions that seem obvious but deepen as the narrative progresses. With its sharp, linear progression of tension, complication and payoff, *Secrets and Lies* is constructed with the kind of craft that is much taught but seldom achieved.

Leigh is a notoriously prickly interview. I learned this in 1992, when I talked to him about *Life Is Sweet*. A question then about his working methods and how long it would take to arrive at a shooting agenda elicited the cryptic dismissal, "Well, a piece of string is as long as a piece of string."

We talk again on a Sunday afternoon, two days after the New York Film Festival premiere of *Secrets and Lies*. As I arrive at his hotel room, Leigh scrambles to pack, hustling to make a plane that will jet him to yet another premiere. Leigh's droopy, sad-eyed face, large eyes peering from above a full salt-and-pepper beard, is preamble to the way he drapes himself over a chair and assumes a comfortable slouch.

"*Naked* was a hard act to follow," Leigh says. "If you make a film where it seems like you deal with everything, what do you deal with next?"

Leigh begins the first of many backtracks and redefinitions that mark his speaking style: "Obviously, A, *Secrets and Lies* deals with a whole load of stuff that's new to me, not least the stuff to do with the adoption. But, B, it is an ongoing preoccupation. *Naked* is not either the conclusive or deviant piece that some people suggest. I mean, it is about family, in the sense it is about people who need to belong, who are disconnected and alienated."

One particularly admirable aspect of Leigh's storytelling is that the wants of the characters, their disappointments, are exposed through the course of the story without ever becoming pathetic. "As a matter of first principle when I create these characters, I do actually like them," he says. "I don't just see them as ciphers. I do believe in them as people. And I deal with what happens in that spirit."

When those characters interact in rehearsal, *Naked* star Thewlis once told me, they go over scenes again and again until they can perform it flawlessly in front of the camera—but in fact the written text never exists until it comes out as transcript. Each scene is learned through building it.

Leigh recounts addressing the ever-present question—How do you arrive at a script?—at a recent Lincoln Center appearance. "In a blinding, clairvoyant flash which I've never actually got together, I said, 'We didn't make a script, we made a film.' And that is the truth of it. In a way, the text is a red herring. My writing is part of filmmaking. I am fussy and particular and relentless about every comma, rhythm of sentence, opposition of words, balance of structure, paragraphs—y'know, tempo, you name it, alliteration, repetition, every literary consideration you can think of. But I remain entirely visual in the way that I operate as a filmmaker."

Silent-film historians contend that movies went downhill when the script was invented. Before that, comedians like Buster Keaton and Harold Lloyd could reshoot endlessly. The script was an instrument of finance, so the producers would know how much money they were on the hook for. But Leigh's style harks back to the silent era. As he says of Feuillade's 1914 French serial *Les Vampires*, "he just got out in the street and made it up."

There are a pair of superlative long takes in *Secrets and Lies* I'm curious about: the major scene in a deserted cafe when biological mother Cynthia (Brenda Blethyn) and daughter Hortense (Marianne Jean-Baptiste) confront their relationship for the first time, with Blethyn moving astonishingly from tears to laughter to tears over eight minutes of screen time; and a barbecue before Cynthia feels compelled to reveal her lost daughter's identity to her family. I wonder when the camera enters the equation.

In the cafe scene, Leigh says, "We did shoot mid-shot singles and close-ups, but when we looked at the dailies the following day—and we only did two takes—the second take was so totally, utterly perfect that we knew straightway without a shadow of a doubt that this was it. But sometimes I shoot close-ups because, not so much you don't think it's going to work, but because you don't know how you'll want the rhythm to go within the overall structure of the film at that point."

The barbecue, then, is portrayed in a sustained take that mingles the strengths of theatre and cinema, with immaculate timing of physical farce and an overlap of the characters sniping at one another. It doesn't literally have plates spinning in the air, but it keeps topping itself, in the style of silent comedy. You think, "How can it keep going? Can it keep going?"

"Well, there was no cover on that shot," Leigh explains. "That *is* the shot. Partly for technical reasons. We had terrible sound problems, very

noisy. As it happens in the end, the scene was mostly post-synched anyway. The light was rushing about. English filming can be desperate because
from one moment to the next the light changes. So this made me think,
'There's all this stuff going on, on a domestic level, with the meal, the
comings and goings. There's a huge network of relationships and on top of
that, the audience is waiting for the shit to hit the fan.' I knew that in the
next scene, when the bomb does goes off, I was going to want to cut a lot.
So that dictated, 'Let's just do it in one shot.'

"In the end," he continues, "there's a level at which you want film to
aspire to the condition of documentary—you want the event to feel like it
really is happening whether you're filming or not. But you also want the
film to aspire to the condition of theatre, or circus. Is he or she going to
fall off the tightrope? The only way to get that to happen is just to be very,
very thorough. [The key to] both scenes, and most of the film, really, is just
rehearsing it all very thoroughly so that the only things that can go wrong
are those things you can't control. You turn on the camera and a steak
suddenly decides that it's a mobile, moving item that jumps off plates. Cans
of beer refuse to open. But the human element is under control!"

In an essay about Ermanno Olmi's 1978 *Tree of Wooden Clogs*, Leigh wrote:
"This remarkable and wonderful film, which I love deeply, is one of the
few true epics. For although it offers neither great romance, nor lengthy
voices, nor wars, nor even death, this masterpiece succeeds effortlessly and
with monumental simplicity in getting to the essence of the human experience. Directly, objectively, yet compassionately, it puts on the screen the
great, hard, real experience of living and surviving from day to day, and
from year to year, the experience of ordinary people everywhere." It's
often said that the best criticism is, in its own way, autobiography.

The ending of *Secrets and Lies* is a quietus, hopeful, more hopeful than
the similar ending to *Life Is Sweet*. In the stark sunlight failing in a boxy
English yard, cramped with sheds and chairs, in a vignette of idealized
domesticity, we can discern the patterns of need and support we have wit-
nessed for more than two hours in only the most contentious form. There
is a moment of calm and Cynthia coos, "Oh, this is the life, ain't it?"

As our time runs out, Leigh takes a last look around the room, then
says, apologetic, "I'm sorry to be in such a rush, but I've got to get to
Canada and that's that."

Mike Leigh

MIRRA BANK/1997

MIKE LEIGH'S SECRETS AND LIES opened this year's New
York Film Festival, fresh from winning the Palme d'Or for best film at the
1996 Cannes Film Festival. Leigh's latest foray into the world of stressed-out
family life was a hit with critics here: "A miracle . . . blazingly funny . . . One
can only respond with tears and laughter together," said David Denby in
New York Magazine, and Kenneth Turan of the *LA Times* wrote, "If film
means anything to you, if emotional truth is a quality you care about, this
is an event not to be missed."

Ironically, despite 20 films to his credit since 1971 (including *Abigail's
Party,* 1977; *High Hopes,* 1988; *Life Is Sweet,* 1991; and *Naked,* 1993), a slew of
festival awards, and retrospectives of his work around the world, as well as
a 1993 OBE award "for services to the British film industry," Leigh has been
snubbed at home by the British Academy of Film and Television Arts, and,
in the U.S., has yet to be approached with serious interest by a Hollywood
studio. Such coolness might signal unease with Leigh's unconventional work
methods, or with his take-it-or-leave-it attitude towards industry power
brokers. But more likely, it's because he has staked out the unglitzy (read:
uncommercial) lower rungs of British family life for his steadfast directorial attention. What's more, when studios hear that Leigh is, in his words
"the guy who works with no script, that there is no casting discussion, no
interference, that I have the final cut . . . that does it," the deal is off and
Mike Leigh remains where he feels most at home: an outsider "auteur," an
intentional misfit.

From *Films in Review,* v. 48. No. 1/2, January/February 1997. Reprinted by permission.

When I first met Leigh at the end of the '60s, I wouldn't have pegged him for a future OBE recipient. I was a student at The London School of Film Technique, then housed in an unheated former banana warehouse on Charlotte Street. My fellow classmate, the future film director, Les Blair, shared a flat with Leigh in Euston. It was a time and place the media dubbed, "Swinging London" — an image of synchronicity that runs counter to my recollection of life there as a random collision of energies. The Who, Cream, or the Rolling Stones seemed to be staging a free concert every time you crossed Hyde Park. Jimi Hendrix was ubiquitous; John Lennon and Yoko Ono were shooting an experimental "pursuit" film with Allan King Associates over on Wardour Street; the Jefferson Airplane touched down for a gravity-and-logic defying concert at the Round House — where Peter Brook and The Living Theatre were also at work exploding the bounds of traditional theatre. All-night screenings were all the rage, and one 12-hour marathon, featuring *Scorpio Rising,* presented Kenneth Anger's entire output, with the filmmaker at the projector providing running commentary. Vanessa Redgrave and Tariq Ali led a massive, chant-driven, Anti-War demonstration through central London to Trafalgar Square; scores traveled to France to take part in "les manifestations de mai," and returned to churn out fliers in support of underground movements in Paris, Berlin, and Prague. Every bed-sit and corner pub harbored Viet Nam deserters, political dissidents, fashion victims, or art-star wannabees from around the world. London was, for that moment, a free-for-all of political disaffection and hip culture.

Then, as now, Leigh was memorable for his testy wit, his deadpan ironies about the Direction of Things in General. He and Les Blair, friends since their years as north England schoolmates, introduced me to the near-hallucinatory humor of writers like Flann O'Brien, and to the anarchic madness of old *Goon Show* radio broadcasts, featuring Peter Sellers, Spike Milligan, and Harry Secombe. Leigh's recent visit here to attend the New York Film Festival premiere of *Secrets and Lies* gave me a chance to get reacquainted and I reminded him of the circumstances under which we'd first met.

MIKE LEIGH: Yes. I knew you through Les. He and I were close buddies, and somewhere along in there he lived in my flat. I had been a student at the London Film School in '64, and later I taught there — '71 to '73. When you and Les were at the film school, I was rehearsing a play next door to the Royal Shakespeare Co. I spent most of the '60s doing theatre, because film wasn't available—but *always* with a view to making films.

Curious about the impact of that time on Leigh's work, I brushed up on his background prior to the late '60s via a recent, authorized biography, *The World According to Mike Leigh,* by Michael Coveney. The book's title suggests Leigh's compulsion to control, not only the agenda of a discussion, but most of the airtime. His hairpin turns, false starts, and qualifications in responding to questions are pre-emptive, sometimes frustrating, but also amusing, and always in service of a higher "truth." Born in 1943 and raised in the environs of Manchester, Leigh is the son of a first-generation Jewish doctor, Abe Leigh, and his wife, Phyllis. Mike attended Salford Grammar, whose other notable alumni include Albert Finney and Les Blair. At Salford, Leigh was an indifferent student and aspiring actor who gained notoriety as a cartoonist. "Less jest, more zest," said one report. By the time he was 12, Leigh had decided to direct films, and he spent much of his teens at the movies or acting in plays. Leigh developed early a skeptical, non-joiner perspective on life through which he filtered from the flood of post-war innovations in literature, theater, and visual arts, those influences that would inform his later work: Pinter, Beckett, Peter Brook, Groucho Marx, the Three Stooges, Picasso, and Cassavetes—to name just a few.

I asked him what "defining experiences" had shaped him as a film-maker...

M L : For me, the most important, seminal experience was the fact that through a fluke, at age 17 (in 1960), I got a scholarship to RADA and trained as an actor in the most sterile atmosphere. And *that* I regard as one of the most fortunate things in my life, because I spent two formative years questioning *everything* in that whole procedure. And beginning to sense other things that were happening.

The collapse of the Old Order and the coming of the Beatles—because by 1967 the Beatles were something beyond being four likely lads from Liverpool...the post-war ferment out of which all of this came—that's to do with our parents' generation being respectable and putting the world together again—whilst we were breaking away. Questioning the Old Order. Certainly that's what I was doing. My notions of how to create film in an organic way—integrating various things together—not least the contribution of actors—came out of a huge number of things...ranging from the Nouvelle Vague, and Cassavetes, the Living Theatre, the Method, Stanislavski, Happenings, Gratowsky. I had an instinct that writing, directing, designing, and filmmaking could all be combined on the floor rather than at the desk.

FILMS IN REVIEW: *Did that late '60s period have any impact on your ideas about how to work?*
ML: No... I'd already invented it three or four years earlier. By that stage I was doing my tenth improvised play—*Bleak Moments*—which became my first film—in 1970.

And though nowhere along the line was anyone doing what I actually turned out to have done—there were all sorts of things that pointed in that direction.... One of the first was *Shadows*—Cassavetes—made in 1959. The discovery that *Shadows* had been in some way improvised was inspirational. I've never regarded Cassavetes as a real influence because I found his work patchy—some of it very fine and some of it extremely tedious—limited to the actors, really—spewing it out—which is the antithesis of what I've been concerned with—getting the essence of the real world. I mean... I am an actor, but a suppressed one, which I think is good. It's good to be a frustrated actor. As a director, as a general condition.

FIR: *Do you remember the Round House?*
ML: Yeah, the Round House... Peter Brook did *Marat/Sade* on stage and I saw a documentary on the box on how the play was all sort of improvisation, coming from research from cases in a mental hospital. It triggered the thought in me that if you could do all that, you could go one stage further and actually make one up.

Of course one of the great curses or diseases of the '60s—in a way—was "Art for Art's Sake." The assumption—that still kind of prevails—that what one is doing is an exercise. You know, the display of experimentation. Whereas for me the real inspiration and the real influences include Vermeer. You know, all art comes out of a progression from there being nothing to the finished thing... a synthesis of improvisation and order. And the only difference is that I share the process with the actors at a different stage from normal in the making of a film.

Leigh became acquainted with The Method, and other Actors Studio techniques, while a student at RADA. But he says the inspiration to develop

films improvisationally came from his work in visual art. Leigh left RADA
to take courses in stage design and film technique; and then life drawing.
At Camberwell Art School, he'd go out with a sketchpad to work from
something real—an approach he'd never encountered in his acting training. His "clairvoyant flash"—that working from the source was the key to
making a work of art—gave Leigh his method as a director. He and his
actors choose a real person from the actor's life, from which they develop
a fictional character in improvisations with other actors whose characters
have been similarly created. The actors are forbidden to discuss their characters or motivations with each other, so none of them have an overview
of the story, none of them are aware of what is going on outside their
scenes. Leigh believes this approach liberates the actor's creativity because
he is freed from pressure to produce "results"—he has only to experience
truthfully what his character is discovering in the moment. As in real life.
From these rehearsals Leigh develops notions from which the story is
"negotiated," and gradually constructed and re-worked over months of
rehearsal. Only at the very end is anything written down...

ML: I had a struggle in the '60s when I was setting up, trying to get projects and things. They'd say, "Well, what do you do?" I'd say, "Well, we've
all worked and improvised this play..." And they'd say, "Oh, you mean a
documentary, because there was documentary theatre. "No, not a documentary," I'd say, "It's a *play*. A dramatic play. You know. Like Chekov."
"No, but didn't you say it was improvised?" "Yeah but it comes out of..."
"Oh, you mean a Happening?" So I carried on doing theater until I could
get to make a film. It was courtesy of Les Blair—who volunteered to produce and edit—that we got *Bleak Moments* made. And courtesy of Albert
Finney, who put up the money.

FIR: *But to work in the way that you do and get the films financed must be
easier now than it was 25 years ago.*

ML: Okay we got *Bleak Moments* made by a complete fluke. That is to say,
Albert Finney gave us the money (£18,000).... But that film was never
supported—I mean I make a film now and it's supported by a whole distribution and media thing, and it gets some attention. *Bleak Moments* won
the Grand Prix at Chicago and Locarno and it was on everybody's "10
best" list all around the world. One immediately thought—"This is it, now
we're on the road to feature filmmaking." But at that time, making proper
grown-up feature films (*Bleak Moments* was a low-budget "cheat" job) was

simply impossible. Indigenous films didn't happen in the U.K. for over a decade after that. Until Channel Four got going (in 1982).

But I was lucky then (1973) . . . I got to go to the BBC and did maybe 11 or 12 films. In that period the BBC was a very positive and rich experience . . . They'd decide on the filming dates, the budgets, and each film had its own project number. And I'd come and they'd say, "Okay those are the dates, that's the project number, this is the budget. Make the film." And that was the end of it. So I made all these films with total freedom. Even on the last one on Northern Ireland (*Four Days in July,* 1984). I mean that film, which after all was a hot potato subject—was never interfered with. Ever. It went out. And I was able to get away with things in Northern Ireland purely because I could plug into this bureaucracy, which I would never have been able to do without the BBC. I mean, I could bail myself out of things, hire cars, and get seats on planes at the drop of the hat. . . .

FIR: *And get your bills paid.*

ML: Yeah. So despite what you may want, I am not (as an independent) able to tell a hard luck story about the difficulty of getting financing, because with these BBC films . . . the only struggle I ever had was, when it came to each new film, persuading a producer to give away one of his or her slots without knowing what [the film] was going to be. So, having been initially conceived, as it were, with *Bleak Moments*—I then spent a long time in the womb, protected, you know—becoming a filmmaker.

FIR: *Building a body of work.*

ML: Building a body of work but also learning how to do it in an ever more sophisticated way. . . . And the fact is that if you made *A Play for Today* as they were called on the BBC, you could be pretty sure you could get eight or nine million viewers in one evening. Now eight or nine million people seeing the film you've just made is not bad. I mean, I don't know how long will it take for eight or nine million people to see *Secrets and Lies* for all its success. It'll take quite awhile.

FIR: *Until it gets on the tube. . . . Was it important to you whether or not these films were released theatrically? Would there have been a different intention?*

ML: I am quite sure that if any of them had been theatrically released, they would have been exactly the same films.

FIR: *Did you have the right to release those TV films theatrically?*

ML: Absolutely not. And I still don't. Even now. They're all out on video. The U.S. is the only country where you can buy them. The BBC won't do a deal for the U.K. in theatrical. There was a general assumption that indigenous British films were simply a no-no. Waste of time. That the proper films—real grown-up films—were "international" (like James Bond fare). Deculturized films. It was very negative and very, very frustrating. The vicious circle was broken by Channel Four starting. But—and this is just my opinion—a large proportion of Channel Four films throughout most of the '80s—although they were independent films and they were successful—they continued, and some still continue, to genuflect towards Hollywood. *The Long Good Friday,* or even for example, *Mona Lisa*—are basically Hollywood genre films. British, and other European filmmaking, has a desire to be what is basically pastiche Hollywood fare. As opposed to what Ozu or Satyajit Ray—or I—would be doing, which is to make a film straight from the scene.

FIR: *What about the "scene?" Does that have anything to do with which of your films have traveled more readily to the U.S.?*

ML: I'd have conversations with potential backers, Americans.... And what I would hear always was the following: "You see, the thing is," they would say, "for a film to work, it has to be successful in the States. And you will never make a film that will ever do anything in the States because they won't understand your films—because your films are television films, and they're domestic." Which I always knew was rubbish, basically. Because I don't make that sort of film.... When we started to make films that we knew could travel I was just thinking about the world, really.

FIR: *Does the fact that your films are now being celebrated in this other context—theatrical cinema, commercial release—have impact on your approach?*

ML: In the most simple and fundamental terms—no it doesn't. But at the same time it would be dishonest and kind of a conceit to say "it-absolutely-doesn't-in-any-way-whatever." I mean over the course of all the work that I have done... It began as uninvited—not low budget—but *no* budget plays where nobody got paid and the set was cobbled together anywhere we could find—for the odd times—three performances or something, late at night. And then to something like *Abigail's Party* (first produced as a play in

1977), which is still my most popular piece in the U.K. Because it happened to go out (on the BBC) on a night when there was a strike on ITV—and something very highbrow on Channel Two—there was no Channel Four yet—and there were storms throughout the U.K. Sixteen million people stayed home and watched. . . . But wherever you tell your story, you have a sense of . . . always, the audience 'round the campfire. . . .

FIR: *Is your work better understood in England or abroad?*
ML: Oh, that is a really interesting question. Sometimes it does seem to be better understood here [in the U.S.], France, Australia, in Germany, and other places . . . I think what that's about is some of the self-loathing and self-deceiving manifestations of English culture.

Perhaps because Leigh's work has had such wide exposure on BBC television, it is universally familiar in his home country, where lurid headlines about domestic life are sometimes characterized as "having the tragedy and farce of a Mike Leigh film." But some critics and opinion makers in England—a society that agonizes over questions of class the way Americans do over race—accuse Leigh of being "patronizing" towards his mostly lower-working class subjects. To which Leigh replies . . .
ML: . . . there is an incredible amount of rubbish that surrounds the perception of my stuff in some quarters which is all to do with not seeing what it actually is . . . or not wanting to acknowledge what it is. For ordinary audiences, people who just get on with it, it's very popular indeed. *Secrets and Lies,* for example, is not a film about class, but you can't make a film in England that doesn't include the class element.

FIR: *What leads in your work? The humanist or dramatic instinct?*
ML: There is a tension, a kind of—how to describe this?—a divergence in my attitude . . . I am drawn to considerable extent to explore the world of the inarticulate and indeed the world of the uneducated. Because I find that important and fascinating and compelling. I've also explored in (more literary) ways, the kind of Beckettian side, all the stream of consciousness stuff. You'll find it all over the place in characters in my films (for example in David Thewlis's "Johnny" in *Naked,* or Timothy Spall's "Aubrey" in *Life Is Sweet*). . . . If I had to say whether it was humanist or dramatic, you'd want me to say it was humanist. But in fact, I'm not so sure that those two

things are particularly divisible, given that we're talking about filmmaking—you know, storytelling. To be honest about this—because that's what you prompted me to do—my history and motivation boil down to two very basic, uncluttered things. One is that I am by nature a storyteller, and that is all there is to it. And secondly, and equally important, is I am by nature a filmmaker. My earliest memories of conceiving stories are in visual film terms. I've never really compromised.

So, while Mike Leigh's origins may be in theatre, his development in 16mm films for TV, and his future in world-class feature filmmaking, his heart appears to remain gyroscopically centered where it's always been: in the daily world that, creatively illuminated, shines with universal truths. Leigh's preoccupation arguably defines the vocation of the independent filmmaker—regardless of budget size, sources of financing, or degree of success. Not to mention his conviction that we as audience should shoulder some of the burden...

ML: All creative process is an investigation that leads to discovering what it is you're doing. That is how artists work...In the end you discover what the film is by making it...And I do believe it's necessary for you to walk away from these kinds of films with questions unanswered, and work to do, and matters to be faced.

Lies Director Shows True Colors

LARRY WORTH/1997

DIRECTOR MIKE LEIGH REFERS to himself as a straight shooter, an assessment that not only proves true but—relatively speaking—puts William Tell to shame.

For instance, take last year's Academy Award ceremony, at which Leigh's most popular film to date, *Secrets & Lies,* was nominated for five Oscars, including best picture, director and script. Most people would say it was an honor to be nominated. But Leigh isn't most people.

"It was a total p--s-off to go home with nothing," he says. "To say otherwise would be bulls--t. It was not, as they say, a nice night out. The thought of going back [if nominated again] makes me feel sick.

"Maybe I'd be a better sport if it had been a straight, clean fight. But we all know it's politics."

And don't get Leigh started on politics, though he's considerably happier with Britain's state of affairs since Labor leader Tony Blair put the Tories' John Major out of a job in May. Aside from Major, he's had plenty to offer about Margaret Thatcher, a favorite target in his scripts.

"Margaret Thatcher is nothing less than a philistine," he says. "Naturally, she doesn't communicate with artists of any kind. So I've got no letter saying she hates my movies. But she's not sophisticated enough for that anyway."

He's equally disdainful about ever going mainstream with his movies. Rather, Leigh wants to keep exploring different aspects of British life in his slice-of-life style, which brings him to *Career Girls* (opening Friday).

From *New York Post,* 5 August 1997. 1997 Copyright, NYP Holdings, Inc. Reprinted with permission from the New York Post.

As the first feature to follow *Secrets & Lies,* one might think pressure was on to produce a hit of equal stature. But Leigh was more concerned with telling a potentially familiar tale—two twentysomething women reuniting six years after college graduation to reminisce on the bad old days—in a new and compelling manner.

Though grounded in reality, the production juggles flashbacks with a number of extraordinary coincidences. And if the public can't relate to those coincidences?

"People who are really bothered by them can clear off," he says. "Let them go live their lives without any sense of humor."

OK, so Leigh's fiercely protective of his oeuvre, but not half as gruff as his sentiments make him sound. A youthful-looking 54, he comes across as a savvy conversationalist, relatively easygoing and open to a good laugh.

He's also open to suggestion, which comes from his unique method of moviemaking, in which he begins a production with a mere concept. Upon hiring actors (most of whom carry limited box-office clout), he then brainstorms the character's entire history, later incorporating them into a script. The results are highly unconventional examinations of life in England.

Not surprisingly, financing used to be an iffy proposition. Moderate hits like *High Hopes* and *Life Is Sweet,* then the much-lauded *Naked,* helped. But the critical and popular embrace of *Secrets & Lies* suddenly made him officially bankable.

"I don't think *Secrets & Lies* was necessarily my best film," he says. "It just took on subjects that resonated: racism, adoption, the whole thing of families, of longing to be connected and belong."

The latter themes certainly ring true for Leigh; though they've parted ways, he remains close friends with actress/wife Alison Steadman, and lives in London with their boys, age 19 and 16. Better still, they double as his best critics.

They'll have their work cut out for them with his next project, a big-budget ($20 million) look at operetta librettist William Gilbert and composer Arthur Sullivan.

"Let's say it won't be a remake of the 1953 bio-pic [*The Story of Gilbert and Sullivan*]," he says with tongue planted firmly in cheek. "I'm attracted to the idea of getting out there and subverting the period movie, the costume drama. But I thought it was about time I did a proper movie. Just for the hell of it."

There's No Face Like Gnome

JOHN NAUGHTON/1997

THE SIGN ON THE staircase leading up to Mike Leigh's office is a
confusing one for those in search of the country's leading independent
film director. Scrawled on a piece of A4 paper in blue felt tip and crudely
taped to the wall, it reads: "Money exchanged on the street cannot be
accepted as payment." Whatever can it mean? Have we mistakenly stum-
bled across some sort of strict, fee-paying, language school, as there are
also signs offering, "French," "oral" and the threat of "corrective discipline." Hmmm.

Located on bustling Greek Street, amid the bright lights of London's
racy Soho district, the offices of Thin Man Films (Leigh and producer
Simon Channing-Williams's company, named in ironic appreciation of
their expanding waistlines) is situated next door to a pub and above a sex
shop, while Leigh shares a staircase with a prostitute. For a man who has
spent a lifetime directing plays and making films about people no one else
was interested in, such surroundings seem appropriately earthy.

Entering Leigh's office, the change in atmosphere is total. Apart from its
location, the place could be mistaken for the sort of domestic setting
which has provided the backdrop to so many of his inimitable dramas. As
you enter, on the right is a little kitchen, then turning left there is Leigh's
desk and beyond that a sort of front room sparsely but tastefully decorated
with TV and video in the corner, a low-level sofa and an even lower chair
in which Leigh sits.

From *Empire* (London), no. 100, October 1997. Reprinted by permission.

Hunched up, hands behind his head, as if surrendering to the enemy, Leigh looks a little like you imagine Gollum might have done if you could ever have been bothered to read *The Lord of the Rings*. A camp actor on meeting a youthful Leigh, remarked, "Ooh, he's very *padded* isn't he?" He had, and still has, a point. Leigh's voice is reedy and youthful, his conversation fast and coherent, yet disjointed, rarely coming in fully formed sentences, and never in polished soundbites. Sometimes he fails to finish sentences in a manner reminiscent of the late Russell "You Are, Are You Not" Harty. Casual, and not smart, in jeans and jumper and occasionally given to scratching the bearded chin which last saw a razor in March 1967, he is two parts unreconstructed '60s bohemian to one part rabbi on his day off. Or an oversized garden gnome, if you will.

Today, he is engaged in the painstaking task of transcribing the text of his latest film, *Career Girls*, for future publication as a screenplay. This involves going through the film, frame by frame, writing down the dialogue and adding necessary directorial annotation. It looks like the sort of dogsbody task that has "work experience" written all over it, but Leigh is adamant only he can do it. And the exercise has proved useful, for repeated viewing has given him a startling insight into his film.

"It suddenly clicked with me. It's actually all right," he enthuses. Perhaps wary of sounding too damn cocksure about the whole thing, he retreats to a more cautious evaluation. "I *think* it's all right. I don't know."

But let no one infer from this that Leigh is a shrinking violet. In his understated world, "all right" is probably the equivalent of another director's "brilliant." Having been warned to expect a prickly customer, *Empire* is on its guard and while Leigh's demeanour is very welcoming, his reputation for not suffering fools gladly is soon confirmed. His conversation is peppered with wheat-from-chaff, character-assessing asides such as "there's a theme running through all of my films — which I'm sure you're familiar with." Thankfully, *Empire*, as you would expect has done its homework. The possibility of being sent up the stairs for "corrective discipline" is, thankfully, averted.

From the excruciating, but compulsive, *Bleak Moments* through the buttock-clenching brilliance of *Abigail's Party* and *Nuts in May*, to his most recent work, Leigh, among other things, has always dealt in that most English of emotions: embarrassment. Does he enjoy embarrassing people?

"I don't think that's the point," he retorts. "I don't like making people embarrassed, I don't think it's anything to do with that really. The point is, that is part of the experience of living."

Suitably chastened (and a little embarrassed), *Empire* suggests that Leigh doesn't generally give much away about himself in interviews and rations out his biographical details rather stingily. Another missed point looms.

"Rationed?" he exclaims indignantly. "You can buy a whole book on it. That's not rationed. For 20 quid you can get the whole story."

Yours, dear reader, for considerably less than 20 quid, the whole Mike Leigh story.

The butterfly effect in *Naked* was explained thus: "Every time a butterfly flaps its wings in Tokyo, this old granny in Salford gets a bilious attack." If Leigh's paternal grandfather, Mayer Liebermann, a refugee from tsarist conscription in Russia, had made his connection on the Hull Liverpool train, he would have made the crossing for New York and there would have been no Mike Leigh. Instead, he missed it and ended up settling in Manchester on the Cheetham Hill Road. In 1939, when German Shepherds started changing their names to Alsatians, the Liebermanns, for obvious reasons, changed theirs to Leigh and four years later Mike was born. After returning from the war, his father, Abe, a doctor, set up as a GP in Cheetham Hill before moving to a more affluent suburb of Salford a decade later.

Leigh was a gifted child, an excellent cartoonist and a natural, and often cruel, wit. Despite these talents, he failed the Manchester Grammar School entrance exam and went instead to Salford Grammar—alma mater of Albert Finney, who co-financed Leigh's first feature film, *Bleak Moments*. At 17, he left Manchester on a scholarship to RADA, whose regime he found suffocatingly antiquated. Was it a depressing experience?

"No, it was a great time," counters Leigh, "because I was 17 and it was 1960 and I got out of Manchester. RADA was repressive enough and sterile enough for me to instinctively confront questions about what we were doing and how we were doing it. It stood as a jumping-off point for what I've been doing ever since."

He enrolled at art school and took an evening class at the London School of Film Technique. It was the first step in his directing career that would take him around regional theatre groups throughout the '60s working on plays with names like *Individual Fruit Pies* and *Glum Victoria* and *The*

Lad with Specs before he released his first feature film, *Bleak Moments* in 1971. Despite being (in Leigh's words) "very slow," *Bleak Moments* received some ecstatic reviews both here and in the U.S. (where it was released under the more upbeat name of *Bleak Moments, Loving Moments*). Roger Ebert, writing in the *Chicago Sun Times* described it as "a masterpiece, plain and simple."

Instead of cementing the success of *Bleak Moments* with a feature film career, Leigh entered limbo, unable to convince potential backers of his films' exportability, crippled by the malaise that afflicted all British directors as the nation's film industry went belly up. Television became his outlet and thanks to maverick producer Tony Garnett (still working in TV, most recently on the excellent *This Life*), he found employment at the BBC. A series of classic TV films followed (*Hard Labour, Nuts in May, Who's Who, Grown Ups*) all of them dealing with Leigh's overriding preoccupations of class, human relationships and communication and establishing his reputation in this country. But does he feel the same way about these films as he does about the ones that gained a cinematic release?

"If you had asked me during any of the 17 years when I—and indeed, everyone else—could only make films for television, I would have given you nothing but bile and violence about this subject. It was really, really choking."

Nowadays, however, Leigh can view the situation with more equanimity, praising the set-up at the BBC which allowed him complete independence and cherishing the quality of the work. With hindsight, he can even muse upon the pitfalls that might have befallen him.

"Even if I had, by some fluke, got a film made during that period with the situation as it was, any number of people would have come along and fucked it up for me..."

This is a quiet time for Leigh as he tries to gear up for the next project. This will be something of a departure, a biopic of Gilbert and Sullivan, the guv'nors of late Victorian light opera, for whom Leigh has nursed a deep affection since compulsory childhood visits to the D'Oyly Carte.

Angered by the leak to the press of his intentions—Leigh generally never comments on any film until it is made—he defiantly promises:

"Anything could happen. It won't be your conventional biopic."

He seems excited by the prospect. Does he like all his films?

"Oh yes. I get extremely cross with filmmakers who say, 'Oh, I hate my films; how can you watch your own films?' That really pisses me off. I don't get it because if you don't like it, how in hell's name can you expect anyone else to? When the NFT shows *Mean Time,* I will go and sit at the back because it will be good to see a print on the screen, it will be good to see it with an audience and I've got a *real* soft spot for *Mean Time.*"

Such affection for his work is also reflected in the way Leigh talks about characters in his films, almost with an implicit belief in their reality and a paternal concern. Talking about Johnny the violent antihero of *Naked* he says: "Plainly, a serious mistake is that Johnny never had a university or college education, a complete bloody waste basically. When he was at school in Manchester, he plainly spent the entire time with people punishing him and throwing him out of the room rather than saying, 'Here is a talent to be nurtured.' "

This deep attachment to characters doubtless stems from Leigh's much-documented working method, where actors discuss with Leigh a number of people they know personally and then settle on one person and pull a story together from their experiences. It's a style which is fundamental to Leigh's stunning originality as a filmmaker, but it has consistently scared off would-be backers.

"We've tried to raise money for various films," remembers Leigh with a sigh, "and they do come along and play games for a while and they *know* there's not going to be a script, they *know* I will not discuss casting and they *know* that I'm going to have final cut. They know it'll probably be all right but they just won't take the plunge. If we were prepared to sell out on these films, we could get much more money than we do. Life would be hell, the spunk would go out of it and then I'd wind up talking to you about a film I can't watch."

It's a safe bet that Leigh will have few problems watching *Career Girls* in years to come. It's the tale of Annie (Lynda Steadman) and Hannah (Katrin Cartlidge), two college friends who meet up for the first time in six years and over the course of a weekend, run into some old acquaintances. It's another impeccably observed, beautifully executed piece, unusual for featuring time shifts, but consistent with Leigh's recurring preoccupations, not least the old men and women thing. Has he reached any conclusions about male-female relationships over his years of inspection and dissection?

Leigh fights shy of generalisations, but finally offers this: "The one kind of formula that you can come down to that cannot be denied some way along the line is that at the most basic level, men can have it off and fuck off, women do carry babies and therefore have to rear them. Therefore men can go on playing games and women have to take life seriously. Now that is deeply dangerous in many ways as a generalisation but nevertheless, it has a fundamental raw truth to it."

Following on from this, there is an obvious line of questioning which needs to be explored. It concerns Alison Steadman, who Leigh met in the Green Room of the Liverpool Everyman Theatre over a bottle of Newcastle Brown, married and had two sons with and who left him for the actor Michael Elwyn. Having rebuffed some basic biographical questions on such neutral figures as Albert Finney and Les Blair and already referred me to the biography, Leigh does not offer much hope that he would answer such questions, and *Empire* is forced to confess that we lack the guts to ask them. A shame, but it wouldn't be a Mike Leigh drama without some unspoken tension would it?

How late did he stay up on election night?

"All night, I went to bed about seven o'clock in the morning."

Did he enjoy it?

"Yeah, without any equivocation, having had all kinds of doubts about the way the Labour Party was going in the past year, oh when it came to the crunch it was just *orgasmic!*"

Empire expresses mild surprise, thinking he might have been too Old Labour to enjoy it.

He leaps forward with a laugh and says, "Okay, here's the alternative answer: I did *not* stay up. As soon as Portillo was defeated I went to bed because I was *so* pissed off, particularly for dear Michael because he's such a great politician and a future prime minister. I was so upset."

Empire offers to print this without mentioning the earlier version.

"Don't you dare," he laughs. "Don't you bloody dare!"

Leigh was invited to the Labour shindig at the Festival Hall, but declined in favour of the couch and a bottle of red. How's he coping with the new level of fame?

"The fact is," he states with a smile, "you don't go into the movies to be obscure, it's just nonsense really. So long as I don't have to dress posh—

obviously you have the same feelings as me on this subject [*cheeky monkey!*] — that's fine. The worst aspect of fame is having to wear a fucking tuxedo which is really tedious, it's awful."

Mike Leigh has come in from the cold but he hasn't wiped his feet. All the same, he can't help being a part of the Establishment, on the jury at Cannes, his films nominated for Oscars. The thought occurs what would the young Mike Leigh make of the 54 year old he has become.

"That's an interesting question," he muses. "To be fair on him I would say, I think what worried him — and still worries his geriatric doppelgänger — was bullshit. Pretentiousness and all of that stuff and people being patronizing. I had enormous respect for people my age and older when I was young if they were upfront and had done it and knew what they were about. Respect is what you earn, really. I think he would have known where it was coming from and I think we can't talk about him any more! I mean, Who does he think he is, anyway?"

Raising Questions and Positing Possibilities: An Interview with Mike Leigh

LEONARD QUART/1997

CINEASTE: *Did you have any idea that* Secrets & Lies *would turn into such a commercially viable and critically praised film?*

MIKE LEIGH: It's curious. I would have thought that *Life Is Sweet* might have received such a response. The truth is, every so often you do a piece of work that manages or happens to hit a nerve or two. Obviously *Secrets & Lies* does just that.

CINEASTE: *Should we assume from the behavior of the characters in the film that the English working and middle classes have less problematic relationships with race than Americans do?*

LEIGH: For me to suggest that racism is absent from English working class or lower middle class life would be a deeply irresponsible assertion. Any hardworking and afflicted Asian shopkeeper will tell you that's not the case. In fact, anybody that's black or Asian will find such a suggestion offensive. The question then arises, why doesn't the family throw up their hands in shock when this black woman, Hortense, materializes and turns out to be Cynthia's daughter? There are several answers. First of all, the fact that racism abounds doesn't mean that it exists everywhere. There are people who just get on with it, and who are used to black people. One of the reasons for seeing Maurice's taking photographs of a wide range of people is to have us understand that this is a guy who deals with a variety of people, and is generally liberal and tolerant.

From *Cineaste*, v. 22, no. 4, 1997. Reprinted by permission.

Also, I wanted to make a film about first-generation black people who are British and black, and who are getting on with their lives in a positive fashion. But the question finally is how do I deal with the racial dimension of the film. In the end I have Hortense show up at the family party, and, of all the things that worry the other people, the fact that she's black is way down on the list of their problems. What happens is that other things have priority, so they accept her. And hopefully that's what happens to the audience as well.

Most people, wherever they're coming from, will start by saying she's a "black person." It's the racism that's inherent in all of us, that we categorize people. Gradually you get to know Hortense as a person, and you forget that she's black. It seems to me that the film makes a good, healthy, old-fashioned statement about racism.

CINEASTE: *You've stated in an interview that most of your characters are not people who can walk off the screen and onto the street—that they are heightened, stylized creations. In* Secrets & Lies, *however, except for Cynthia, the characters are essentially naturalistic.*

LEIGH: Yes, she is relatively more stylized than the other characters. The critic of *The Los Angeles Times* once wrongfully said that *High Hopes* exhibited a diversity of acting styles. It seems to me that my films have a great consistency of acting styles, but exhibit the kind of diversity of behavior that occurs in real life and among real people. I don't actually think it's remotely accurate to describe Brenda Blethyn's acting as being stylistically any different from anybody else's in the film. The character of Cynthia is just behaviorally more complex, and therefore, if you choose to view her in terms of acting styles, it's possible to misread it.

My point is that no work of art is truly naturalistic. Art is not real life, and has to be organized, designed, and distilled because it's dramatic. There is nothing accidental, it's all contrivance.

What is real is a very complicated, epistomological question. The fact is that none of *Secrets and Lies* is actually reality. The scene in the café between Hortense and Cynthia, with its rows of empty tables, is the most brazen piece of dramatic license in the film. Where would you find a completely empty café in London's West End? It's as stylized as the expressionist-style shot of Johnny standing alone in the dark in the homeless encampment in *Naked*. There are a number of shots like that in *Secrets & Lies*, where the images work on different levels. For example, the montage of photo sessions provides a quite heightened combination of images, all of them subtly, or maybe not so subtly, trying to arouse audience response.

CINEASTE: *What do you want the audience to feel about Maurice's wife, Monica? She seems unpleasant—obsessed with shopping, the decor of her house, and social status, and, in her startled reaction to Hortense, guilty of genteel racism.*

LEIGH: Her response to Hortense is based on the fact that it's a Sunday, and she's black and dressed in black. She simply thinks that Hortense is a Jehovah's Witness. I think if you read Monica right, she suffers not only from her infertility but also from menstrual cramps, so she's filled with anxiety. But in the film's final sequence you see her capable of behaving in a warm and sympathetic way. I want her to be seen as a multifaceted character.

CINEASTE: *I thought the opening funeral scene in* Secrets & Lies *contained extremely fluid camera movement. Have you decided to use a moving camera more in your films?*

LEIGH: It's a bit of a myth that my camera is essentially stationary. I take pride in my camera movement. What critics are confused by is my antipathy to being gratuitously virtuosic. The camera in my films always does what it should do—whether it is as static as in the cafe scene in *Secrets and Lies* or as mobile as it is in the opening scene of *Naked*. In that scene I suggested to my cinematographer, Dick Pope, that he put the camera on his shoulder and run with the action. I felt it would be jagged and rough, and set the tone for the film. I think it worked. So it's important to me what the camera does, but it's not the same as indulging in gratituous pyrotechnics.

CINEASTE: *From the opening funeral scene on, the film is touched with a sense of the death of parents and the difficulty of our ever making a true connection with them.*

LEIGH: A major aspect of what the film is about is the relationship of parents and children. It's a film about our need for parents, and our pain about their loss. And what I wanted to capture was the complex nature of these connections. For example, Hortense speaks about loving her adopted mother, and how good she was, but also that she never really spoke to her, and that she got on her nerves. I'm looking to get at the truth of these relationships without making an American-style film where everything is spelled out. I also try not to suggest that there is an unambiguous, fixed truth inherent in these relationships that can be conveyed. I want my films, in a Talmudic way, to raise questions and posit possibilities.

CINEASTE: *Are you becoming less skeptical and more sanguine about the nature of human relationships?*

LEIGH: I reject the implicit suggestion that I'm more optimistic now than when I directed *Naked*. I still feel as despondent about what the world will be like in 2030. Apart from that, on a quite different level, the fact is the older you become, the milder and more multifaceted one's view gets. I think, however, when you ask a question like this I'm forced to think back to earlier films I made like *Bleak Moments* and *Hard Labor*. The general memory of *Bleak Moments* was of a kind of relentless emptiness. But, actually, for a film made by a twenty-eight-year-old, there is a lot of compassion, warmth, love, and understanding of relations inherent in it. It wasn't any less compassionate than *Secrets & Lies*.

INDEX